MY WORLD CUP

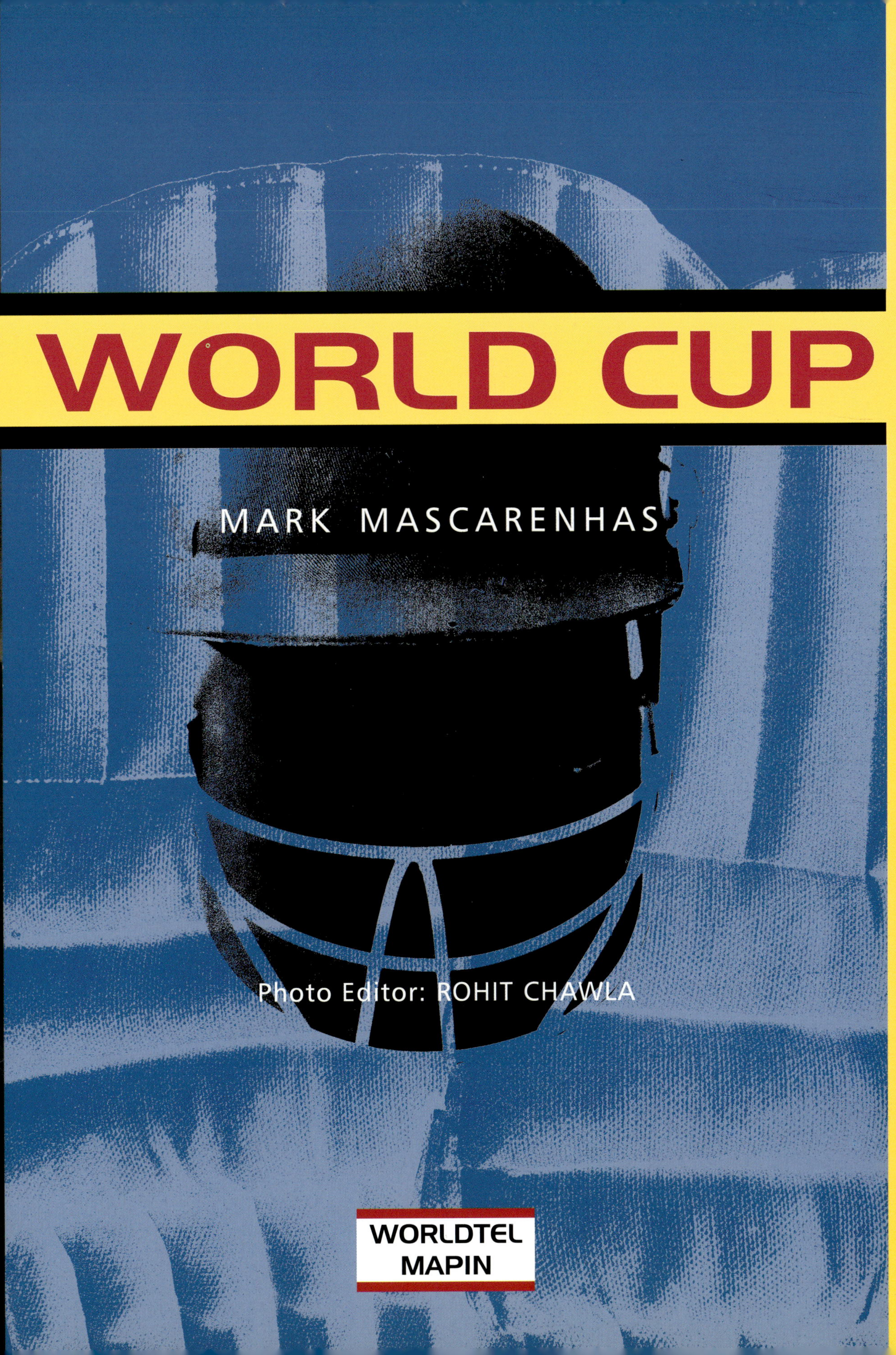

MARK MASCARENHAS

Photo Editor: ROHIT CHAWLA

WORLDTEL
MAPIN

First published in the
United States of America
in 1997 by
Grantha Corporation
80 Cliffedgeway
Middletown NJ 07701

in association with
WorldTel Sports India Pvt. Ltd.
338, 1st Main Road, Cambridge Layout
Ulsoor, Bangalore 560008 India
and
Mapin Publishing Pvt. Ltd.
31 Somnath Road, Usmanpura
Ahmedabad 380013 India

Edited by Vivek Menezes
Designed by Jatin Banker/
Mapin Design Studio
Colour separation by Reproscan
Printed in Singapore

ISBN: 81-85822-49-2 (Mapin)
ISBN: 0-944142-34-6 (Grantha)
LC: 97-71687

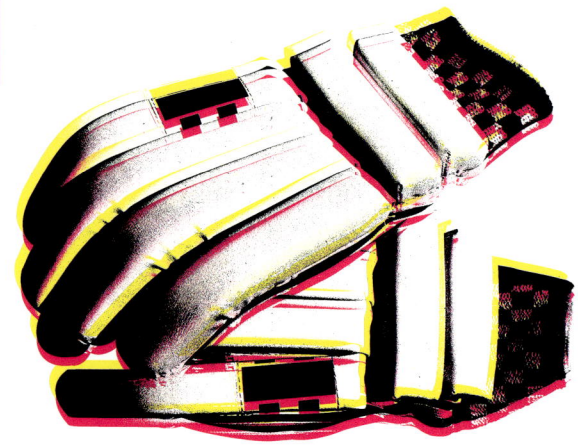

To my wife Karen for her encouragement, endurance and support

CONTENTS

ACKNOWLEDGEMENTS

This book and my entire career would not have been possible without the contributions of my parents Gerry and Marie Mascarenhas who made me what I am and have always been unqualified in their enthusiasm about my professional success.

My sister, Jeanne-Marie Boga, came on board in December 1995 and was of great assistance in relieving me of some of the pressure as we came down-to-the-wire in our preparations.

Gary Franses, the Executive Producer, made it happen in the land of chaos thanks to his methodical and meticulous planning and execution. Neil Harvey, the Technical Producer, was the man responsible for assembling all the technical components; he managed over 80 tons of camera and satellite equipment and miles and miles of cable — and made it all work without one technical hitch. Joanna Lewis, the Production Manager, planned and controlled the movements of our entire operation and made sure that 200 crew members got to where they were supposed to be.

The members of the Grand Slam Sports Board, Alan Pascoe, Edward Leask, Ron Allison and Derek Brandon, who got together with me to win the World Cup. My television network clients, John Knowles; Adam Singer, Bruce Smith and Trevor East; K.P. Singh Deo and R. Basu; Lynton Taylor, David Leckie and Gary Burns; Robin Kempthorne; Majid Khan; Gary Davey, Kelly Butler, Andrew Carnegie and Gene Swinstead, who all had faith that our team would be able to pull it off.

My legal advisors, Soli Sorabjee, Steve Salorio, Julia Palca, Zia Mody and Sajjan Mehta, for all the excellent advice which prevented anyone from taking the contract away from me.

Kerry Sweeney and Mary Scanlon for their efforts during the years of preparation and for holding the fort in Connecticut during my numerous trips to the subcontinent.

My colleagues, friends and family in Bangalore, who were always ready to lend a helping hand.

Foreword by **Mark Mascarenhas**

Bangalore, March 9 1996
What a night it was! My hometown, my family and friends around me, the most exciting match I have ever seen developing in front of us.

The World Cup quarter-finals, India was beating Pakistan in front of an enthusiastic crowd. As the stands erupted to celebrate victory and the sounds of revelry enveloped the entire Garden City, I looked around me and saw my wife Karen, my sister Jeanne and brother Borys, and my friends Viv Greig, Adi and Parmesh Godrej, Vijay Mallya and Jonathan Mermagen and realised that this was success, everything else from that moment onwards would never be quite as meaningful. I had returned to my hometown after almost twenty years away, and this moment belonged partly to me.

I knew that this vital cricket match, one of India's finest hours, was partly my doing.

This is the story of the historic 1996 Cricket World Cup, the greatest tournament in the history of the game. This is also my story, a narrative that begins in my office in Connecticut and ends at the spectacular 1996 World Cup Final with Sri Lanka emerging as Champions of the World.

This book is not meant to be an official publication or a treatise on cricket. Rather, it reflects my experience of this unforgettable event. You will read about how I became involved with the 1996 World Cup, and how my company, WorldTel Inc., managed to pull off a feat never achieved before.

That is my story, told from my perspective. Great global events, however, have unique impacts on each individual involved, and after all nearly a billion people watched their favourite cricket teams compete in the 1996 tournament. To add to my story, I have invited some of my friends to talk about their experiences at the 1996 World Cup.

Cricket fans will recognise all of the names, I am glad to say that all of them believe that the 1996 World Cup set a standard for the future. All of them report indelible memories from those weeks in the subcontinent, and each and every contributor to this book has given us a glimpse of his inner feelings as the world's best cricketers battled for supremacy.

You will feel Imran Khan's disappointment as his team bowed out in Bangalore, you will rejoice with Sunil Gavaskar over the subcontinent's success in putting together a tournament like this across thousands of miles and three countries. You will read about the most exciting matches, the most thrilling upsets and the greatest innings played. And you will learn about the manoeuvrings that took place behind the scenes before the world's best cricket players could face off on the field.

My journey to that unforgettable night in Bangalore began in Connecticut, in the spring of 1993. WorldTel was in the midst of representing the United States Soccer Federation which was a year away from hosting the 1994 Soccer World Cup and cup fever had hit me! I heard that the next Cricket World Cup was going to be held jointly by India, Pakistan and Sri Lanka. I became very interested very fast.

I didn't know it at the time, but the path I was embarking on was to lead to three years of the most intense and challenging experiences of my life. The battle began in August 1993.

After a long and intense struggle, cloaked in all of the business intrigue of the region, WorldTel signed a contract with the World Cup organising committee (PILCOM) on August 21. Once again, we were in the right place at the right time with the best cash offer. But we almost didn't make it.

TSL (Television Sports and Leisure) was favoured heavily by the Pakistan Cricket Board, TWI (Trans World International) was backed by the Indian officials. But WorldTel offered PILCOM $10 Million, the largest offer they had received. Things looked bleak when our offer was topped at the last moment by TSL, but their bid turned out to be unsecured.

The 1996 World Cup was mine!

There was no time to celebrate our underdog victory over regional politicking. Our offer to PILCOM was widely considered to be foolhardy and a very serious financial risk. My competitors openly predicted that I would be quickly forced out of business thanks to the Cup deal... But I just wouldn't quit.

I had never sold a cricket event before, but I had plenty of experience marketing sports television all over the globe. I also knew the most important fact about cricket: there was a lot of competition in each individual market. In England and India, and in Australia, New Zealand and South Africa, competing television networks were fighting hard to win a market share.

It was clear that the 1996 World Cup was going to be a cherished prize in the world market. But was it going to be

Top: *Vijay Mallya and Jeanne getting to their seats at the India Pakistan match in Bangalore.*

Bottom: *Celebrating India's victory, Vivian Greig congratulates Parmesh Godrej.*

rich enough a prize to justify the biggest gamble of my life? My critics said No! But I persevered...

It took two months to finalize the first deal, with Television New Zealand (TVNZ). It was a very tough period personally. It actually felt a lot more like two years!

I have always considered the first deal the most significant because it sets the pattern for what is to follow, even if it is not the most significant in dollar terms. The pattern came true in this case.

For the first time in the history of television in New Zealand, TVNZ had lost coverage of their national cricket team to competitor TV3. TV3 had the rights to broadcast the New Zealand tour of Australia in 1993, and TVNZ was anxious to consolidate its position. I was ready to make a deal and so was John Knowles, TVNZ Director of Sport. He flew to New York and it didn't take very long for us to sign an agreement.

TVNZ agreed to pay $1.95 million for the New Zealand television rights, several hundred percent more than the sum they had paid to secure the rights for the previous World Cup. The hunt was on...

In September 1993, I had lunch with Chester English and Jay Stuart. Chester is a friend and business partner of mine. In 1992 we had successfully orchestrated a takeover of the Alpine Ski World Cup circuit in Europe. Jay represented Kagan World Media, the world's leading television industry analyst and was interested in learning about my recent cricket acquisition.

After a bottle or two of wine followed by cognac and cigars, which he decided to sample after watching Chester and me enjoy ourselves, Jay claimed that he had a buyer for the TV

rights to the World Cup in England. That evening he called my suite at the Ritz Hotel and left a message with my wife to say that his client was extremely serious about making a bid. This lead was for real.

Less than a month later, I met Jay again. We met in the dark downstairs library of Blakes Hotel in London. This time, we were joined by Bruce Smith of Telewest, a member of the UK cable consortium CPP-I.

By Christmas that year, we had hammered out a deal in principle. CPP-I would pay WorldTel $7.5 million for the exclusive World Cup television rights in the UK. With the first two deals, I had nearly made back the money guaranteed to PILCOM, and WorldTel still had the rest of the world to sign up. As far as I was concerned, the game had begun!

In November, I was invited to Calcutta by Jagmohan Dalmiya, who in addition to being convenor-secretary of the World Cup organising committee was the President of the Cricket Association of West Bengal. The Association was celebrating its diamond jubilee and had organized a commemorative cricket tournament sponsored by Hero Honda, (an Indian manufacturer of two-wheelers) featuring India, Zimbabwe, South Africa, West Indies and Sri Lanka.

The Hero Cup was the first international cricket event I had attended since I left Bangalore in 1977. It was also my first visit to the fabled Eden Gardens in Calcutta. I will never forget

Top: **Jagmohan Dalmiya, Convenor/Secretary of the World Cup and Tony Greig at the ground in New Delhi.**

Bottom: **Madhavrao Scindia, President of Pilcom, and Inder Bindra, Indian Cricket Board president, unveil the Wills World Cup mascot, 'Googly'.**

that moment, it rekindled my boyhood passion for cricket...

India played South Africa in the semi-finals, and won dramatically in the final over as the boy-wonder Sachin Tendulkar took the ball in an amazingly gutsy move. The home team then went on to annihilate the highly favoured West Indies in the finals.

Meanwhile, cricket in India was in utter turmoil. Television coverage of the Hero Cup was in disarray, the event almost went up in smoke. The Information and Broadcasting Ministry refused to provide TWI (a WorldTel competitor) with the right to uplink their video signal. TWI had gone ahead and sold the television rights to Rupert Murdoch's Star TV. The Indian national network (Doordarshan) had been left out in the cold and the government network was enraged. At the very last minute, the Indian courts intervened and allowed both Star and Doordarshan to televise the event.

The Information and Broadcasting Ministry remained firm in its position about not granting anyone other than Doordarshan a satellite uplink for the World Cup.

The issue of the uplink was front page news all across India for the next few months. Indian Cricket Board officials felt that if Doordarshan did not allow foreign organisations to uplink, the World Cup would be moved to Pakistan and Sri Lanka. The response from the Information and Broadcasting Ministry was that granting a foreign organisation the right to uplink would be a threat to national security and India's own sovereignty.

Uplink is a similar process to a downlink. Imagine a dish antenna on top of a building or home that pulls signals in from space bringing pictures into the home. Uplinking is exactly the reverse — the signal is transmitted from a point on earth, i.e. the match site, utilising a similar (though more sophisticated) dish, onto a satellite from where the signal can be received by end users. Governments like the U.A.E. (and many European nations until recently) continue not to allow anyone other than the government organisation to uplink. Their justification for this policy is that national security needs to be preserved. The real reason why governments do this is to protect their own monopolies i.e. Etisalat in the U.A.E. or PTCL in Pakistan. These monopolies are then able to charge exorbitant tariffs to the user.

With the ongoing unrest in Kashmir, no one could challenge the Information and Broadcasting Ministry's claim...

I remember meeting R. Basu, the Doordarshan director-general, for the first time at PILCOM President Madhavrao Scindia's home in New Delhi. He was absolutely adamant; Doordarshan was going to buy all of the equipment and produce the World Cup. WorldTel could assist them.

This stance was more amusing than anything else. I knew that Doordarshan's position was untenable because the kind of equipment necessary to cover the World Cup, and the number of production units that needed to be deployed, would cost over $50 million. Besides, the government had in place a new policy to hold everyone accountable and Doordarshan's expenditure far exceeded its income.

Just two months later, in May 1994, I was officially summoned to India's capital city. This time, the Prime Minister's office had begun to intervene; it was clear to everyone involved that a deal had to be made. I met with Basu again, and this time he was all charm and very persuasive. He said that Doordarshan would give me whatever sum I wanted to get the rights to the World Cup.

I pulled the figure of $5 million out of my hat and he accepted it. (Later, the fee would drop marginally to $4.75 million in order to accommodate a small concession requested by the I&B Minister). Doordarshan had signed a record deal!

The full significance of the Doordarshan deal had nothing to do with the dollars involved. As a proud Indian I realised that despite general unhappiness over their national network, no Indian would ever want to see Doordarshan trashed by a foreign company. Now, with the 'jewel in the cricket crown' firmly in its grasp, India's national network was back in the midst of things. And WorldTel was being applauded for siding with the national government rather than with the foreign satellite operators.

The summer of 1994 brought yet another twist to the story. Inder Bindra, President of the Indian Cricket Board, appeared determined to promote an ESPN deal which was being brokered by TWI. Under the terms of the agreement, ESPN would get the television rights to all domestic and international cricket that took place in India for five years.

In business, normally a tender is issued and companies are invited to submit bids. The most beneficial offer is then accepted. This is not what happened that summer. The Board signed a deal for five years at a sum that even then, was not very impressive. Considering that the TCCB had recently signed a television deal for $22.5 million per year, the ESPN arrangement with the Board giving it $2 million a year, while

Top: **Unit A's Mike Turner and Ruth Heyman get ready for the pitch report while a technician fixes the stumpcam watched by Technical Producer, Neil Harvey (extreme right).**

Bottom: **The first world class jumbo TV screen in the subcontinent, installed in Wankhede stadium in Mumbai.**

5 million for its services,

ey claimed that they were
the rights. When ESPN's
satellite went down, it
that the West Indies tour
oordarshan moved the
coming West Indies tour
ons of avid cricket fans
em the right.

e for the World Cup,
to assist them in the
We worked with a crew
han technicians, and we
perb, never-seen-before
ndard.

e whole country seemed
reciation of their effort.

s Azhar checks out Mark

stan contest, Intikhab Alam
l at the pitch.

e pre-match tension with

r Doordarshan covering the

mentary team with Mark
field Sobers, Glenn Turner,
taudi, Ravi Shastri and Kris

Every front page of every newspaper hailed the national network as a superb broadcaster, using superlatives that had never before been applied to Doordarshan.

In the end, my alliance with Doordarshan cost me, personally, over a million dollars in penalties from the Cricket Board. But I will tell you, that alliance was a personal accomplishment that satisfied me greatly. I rank it second only to the World Cup itself as my most meaningful professional achievement.

We succeeded in taking a much-reviled network that was down in the dumps over its dismal cricket coverage and turned it overnight into a world-class broadcaster, capable of the highest standards. The success of the West Indies Tour gave me the confidence that we could accomplish our ultimate mission. It's one thing to dream up a world-class plan with all of the best technical components available — it is another thing entirely to actually get the opportunity to stage a rehearsal and come out with flying colours.

We spent the first few months of 1995 planning the production of the World Cup. The executive producer Gary Franses, the technical producer Neil Harvey and the administration manager Joanna Lewis worked hard under enormous pressure from PILCOM to deliver what was clearly going to be a $5 million production for less than $4 million.

Convincing officials about the actual costs involved was probably the hardest job I had in preparing for the World Cup. PILCOM always felt that I wasn't being hard enough on the producer, to pressure him to cut his budget down. This would end up having a telling effect on my relationship with the producer, who in turn felt I wasn't standing up enough for him.

The task of producing 37 matches in three different countries (two of which were on the verge of war) was difficult enough.

by transport plane. The schedule of the World Cup matches, with an allowance for a rain day for each match, made it impossible for commercial aircraft to do the job.

The production budget negotiations with PILCOM continued on into the summer. And the countdown to the World Cup began in earnest. WorldTel saw that Doordarshan was stalling us on executing a detailed contract, and after several warnings we terminated our relationship. Star TV came on board. Over the next three months, we fought it out fiercely in the courtroom.

While all these distractions were taking place, the preparations for the World Cup went on unabated and on a war footing. We were finalizing hotel and travel arrangements and hiring close to 200 technicians, chartering IL-76 aircraft, assembling the commentary team, and scrambling to gather the countless official permits required to go ahead.

The Indian press started to publicly question whether the vast domestic television audience of avid cricket fans would even get to see the cup. They openly said that the domestic broadcast was in jeopardy because of the Doordarshan/ WorldTel problem. I never gave a moment's thought to any negative possibilities. My team and I were working at full-pitch, 20 hours and more a day.

In January 1996, we received some vindication through the courts. Judge Pandit, of the Delhi High Court, delivered his verdict. In a 37-page judgment, he blasted Doordarshan for its stance, severely criticised Doordarshan officials for their conduct in the matter and upheld WorldTel's decision to terminate its relationship with the national network. In the final piece of drama, just a week before the first match, we settled on an out-of-court settlement resuming our original co-production agreement.

t the 17 matches in India
rent venues across the
ix venues, and Sri Lanka

uate infrastructure of
e conventional Outside
round as we might have
ngham and London or
l Washington D.C. We
y-away kits (where each
s packed into suitcases)
s and equipment around

aj Singh, Hon. N.K.P. Salve,
Tagore, Amrit Mathur.

While all the final arrangements were falling into place, a customs officer in Ahmedabad was refusing to let our equipment out of his custody. Obviously the news hadn't trickled down from New Delhi or he hadn't read the newspapers that Doordarshan and WorldTel had mended fences and were now co-producing the World Cup matches in India.

Our TV networks were excited and ready: TVNZ in New Zealand, CPP-I/BSkyB in the UK, Doordarshan in India, PTV in Pakistan, SLRC in Sri Lanka, 9 Network in Australia, SABC/M-NET in South Africa, BTV in Bangladesh, Star TV across Asia and broadcasters across North America. We were going to be broadcasting live to a potential audience in excess of a billion people and three years of intense hard work had led us to this moment.

I wound up being involved in every single aspect of the preparations for our production.

There were cost considerations to take into account, and I had to supervise the chaos of trying to book and pay for accommodations and travel for over 150 people. At the last minute, I was negotiating for Super-Slo-Mo technology to be utilised in our broadcasts despite the fact it was not included in our original budget. (This technology turned out to be one of the greatest advancements in cricket broadcasting, fast becoming a fan favourite. For the first time, viewers sitting at home could see the intricacies of spin on the cricket ball as it left the bowler's hand and pitched up at the batsman).

I was successful in persuading Philips to pay for and provide the finest state-of-the-art graphics for our telecast, ensuring that television viewers would receive broadcasts of the very highest world standard.

In the end, I had to be involved in the smallest nuances of our broadcasts; the commentators, blazers and official ties, and even the details of our own crew clothing. For these, we used Kent and Curwen, traditional sports outfitters for blazers and ties, and had more made by Prestige Tailors in Bangalore. The latter was chosen because of the owner, Noaman Razak's persistence. He showed up at my office everyday and waited patiently to be called in with 'Master', his expert cutter. Noaman always nodded his head, claiming that anything could be done and ready by the next day. When we travelled to Calcutta, Noaman and his team followed us and set up shop in a large room adjacent to the grand ballroom.

It was here, in the grand ballroom, that the ICC circus took place when Australia and the West Indies insisted that they would be unsafe if they played as scheduled in Sri Lanka.

As this episode played out, I felt sad for Jagoo Dalmiya. This World Cup was his baby and after all the hard work he had put in, it appeared there was a real chance that his dream was falling apart. Jagoo simply wouldn't accept 'no' for an answer; he gave the West Indies and Australia team managers all the assurances under the sky to persuade them to rethink their decision. Unfortunately the decision had already been made back home. Jagoo didn't rest that entire night; he tried every possible angle.

That evening, at the WorldTel cocktail reception on the lawns of the Taj Bengal, we were summoned by him one by one to where he stood across the pool to try and find a way to convince the West Indies to play in Colombo. His strategy was right; if the West Indies would go, then Australia would be forced to join them. Unfortunately, the West Indies did not change their minds and the tournament lost what would become two very important preliminary matches. Sri Lankan board members Ana, Hilary and Anura, also were trying desperately to convince their cricket colleagues that they would be protected.

I had been in Colombo when the bomb went off in January. I was there to ensure that production plans were on schedule and also to see my client Singer who were going to sponsor the Singapore tournament I was going to televise immediately after the World Cup. It was terribly sad to see the entire city in shock. There weren't enough fire engines and ambulances available to cope with a catastrophe of this size. Poor innocent victims were being rushed to hospital in the cars of private citizens who were trying to help their fellow countrymen.

With the Australia and West Indies matches lost, the Sri Lankan Cricket Board was really being hit hard. When the bid to bring the World Cup had been submitted, Sri Lanka opted out of any financial risk so now they had no share of sponsorship and television profits. All they had as their share were the four matches to be held in Sri Lanka and the television rights to those matches for the territory of Sri Lanka only. They had now lost two of these important four matches.

Top: **The India West Indies television commentary team photographed before the match.**

Mark Mascarenhas

The Eden Gardens, Calcutta: February 11,1996.

The World Cup was officially under way and its first few hours were a complete disaster. The producer of the opening ceremony, who had been brought in from Italy, collapsed in fright at the last minute. He had promised far more than he was capable of delivering. The compere, Indian actor Saeed Jaffrey, appeared ignorant of cricket and quite disinterested. He was unable to distinguish the South African from the Zimbabwe side. For some reason, he seemed far more interested in telling the assembled audience that he had acted in David Lean's "Passage to India".

The Indian press was merciless, showering an unrelenting barrage of criticism on the first event of the World Cup. All of a sudden, I started to feel that my unending efforts over the past three years were on the line. The same press which had hyped my performance to that point looked ready to tear me apart if I could not deliver the goods.

I never stopped working towards a world-class performance. After the opening ceremony I was so excited that I couldn't sleep before our telecast of the first match in Ahmedabad two days later.

The first telecast went off without a hitch. New Zealand upset England in a well-played cricket match. Unit A, one of two in India, performed well. I was satisfied with our first effort, and set off to Hyderabad to watch Unit B begin their effort.

The night before the West Indies match against Zimbabwe, all of the team gathered in my hotel suite. I met Rob Sherlock and Graham Koos from Australia's Channel 9 for the first time. Tony and Viv Greig were there, as were Sunil Gavaskar, Kris Srikkanth, Kirti Azad and Simon Reed. My old friend from Connecticut, Ken Richards, joined us as did Neil Harvey, the man with complete responsibility for all of the awesome technical logistics involved in our production plans.

Sherlock and Koos analysed Unit A's performance from the previous match and began telling us how they could improve their coverage. Their analysis sounded great, but as Simon said to me 'they can sure talk a good game but let's see how they perform tomorrow.'

Boy did they perform!

Sherlock showed himself to be an absolutely brilliant director of the action. He showed the millions of avid cricket fans across the subcontinent what great cricket coverage could be. He showed them close-ups of the players constantly, batting, bowling and fielding. No one in the region had ever seen such compelling television coverage of cricket. His videotape replay man, Newt, who was also from Australia was another revelation. He might have looked like a long-time hippie just off the boat from Goa, but he was raring to go. And he was brilliant. His duty, the video replay section is a vital component of a cricket telecast. Newt was the man who decided which camera offered the very best review of the play called by the Director. All through the tournament, Newt's performance was nothing short of great, he gave Rob exactly what he wanted.

And our telecasts started to get rave reviews from around the world.

In covering cricket, often networks utilise their own individual commentary teams working side by side with a team for a world feed. But before the Cup had begun, I had presented the concept of having one commentary team, featuring the finest in the world, for all my television network licensees. Our line-up was a cricket broadcaster's dream team. It was the most impressive commentary roster ever seen in the game with luminaries like Richie Benaud, Tony Greig, Ian Chappell, Sunil Gavaskar, Imran Khan, Ravi Shastri, Geoff Boycott, Michael Holding, Asif Iqbal, Tony Lewis, Bob Willis, Richard Hadlee, Keith Stackpole, Ranjit Fernando and Lee Irvine.

We got to know each other really well over those weeks, I spent a great deal of time with my commentators. One thing I can tell you is that, as Ravi put it after his first stint on the air with Richie Benaud during the India/West Indies match, Benaud is King!

Greigy was superb as the front-man for each telecast. His pre-game shows were a tremendous success and he worked very hard to ensure it. I suppose he was the perfect host for the World Cup. A South-African born (you can still detect the accent) former captain of England, he is a well-known television commentator in Australia. On the subcontinent, he is wildly popular for his feats as a cricketer as well for his career as a commentator.

With dramatic competition taking place in every match, and while watching teams struggle to outdo each other, our production units started to get into the act. With 5 production units operating during the World Cup, (A'B in India, C'D in Pakistan and a WorldTel/SLRC unit in Sri Lanka), I suppose that inter-unit rivalry was bound to start up.

Gary Franses was not only the Executive Producer of the entire production for the World Cup, he was director of Unit C in

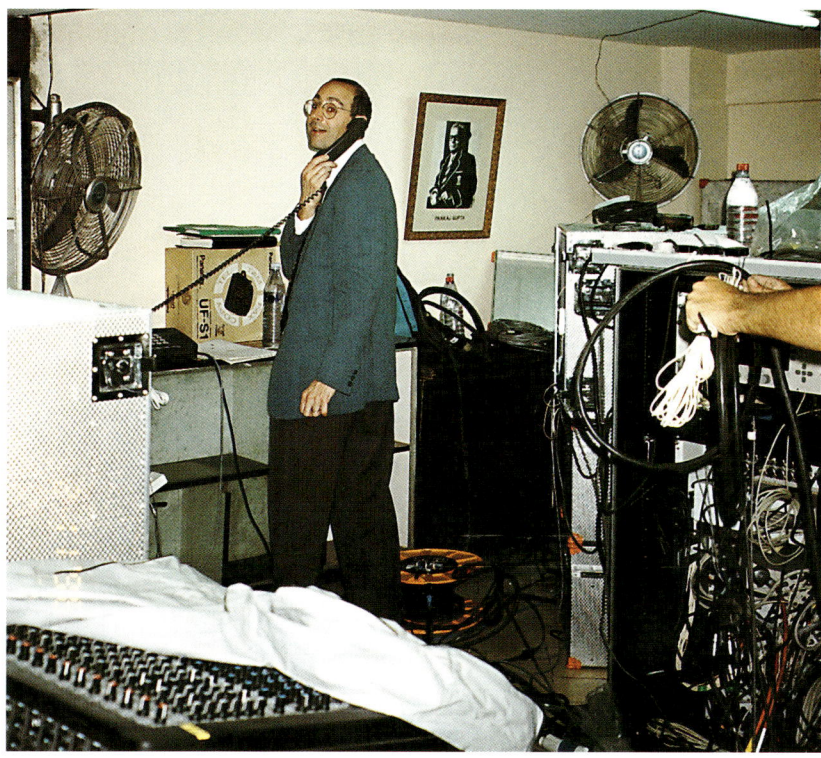

Top: **Gary Franses, the executive producer in the control room in Calcutta.**

Bottom: **A convoy of decorative trucks in Pakistan - transporting TV equipment from the airport to the stadium.**

Pakistan. Gary chose to direct this unit because it would be this Unit C that would cover the final in Lahore and it was his dream to direct a World Cup final!

We'd speak nearly every day to talk about what the coverage was looking like and to discuss various problems or any changes or adjustments that needed to be made with the production. We had taken great care in selecting the commentary team and then went further to discuss the specific pre-match and post-match assignments — which commentator would open the telecast, which would do the pitch report and captains' interviews and who would host the Man of the Match presentation.

I remember Gary telling me one day that he wished he was directing in India because the stadiums there were packed and the crowd atmosphere made the television presentation so much more compelling.

The producer of Unit A, John Bodner of the BBC, took great pride in producing what we call 'prettys' — charming vignettes of the city where the match was taking place. We used these in the opening of each match telecast. The programme would begin with a map of India and then we zero in on the location of the city in question, then take viewers on a brief, colourful, sightseeing tour. I watched every match telecast very closely and then would call the producer/director in the control room of the match venue with my comments on the quality of the telecast. I thought John's material on Gandhi Ashram, in Ahmedabad, was outstanding, as were his vignettes on New Delhi.

In the second week of March, the elimination rounds started. It was then that the ultimate happened: India had to play Pakistan in my hometown of Bangalore. Anyone who grows up in the subcontinent as I did, knows that there is no cricket action in the world which compares to the drama that always ensues when India and Pakistan play each other.

Two days before the match, Sherlock and Koos met up with me for a drink, to discuss the upcoming telecast of the India/Pakistan match. We had a unique problem on our hands. Normally there are 5 commentators on the broadcast team for a cricket match — this time we had 7; Benaud, Chappell, Greig, Gavaskar, Shastri, Imran and Ahmed. Koos and Sherlock wanted me to drop at least one.

I decided we needed to have the four commentators from the subcontinent in order to maintain the balance between India and Pakistan. I wanted the three Channel 9 network commentators as well because the world audience was very familiar with their voices and I could utilise them to project the excitement that was going to be felt in the subcontinent, across Australia, England and the rest of the world.

In the end, the viewers loved our coverage of the India/Pakistan match. We had no complaints about our star-studded commentary team, which sported an unheard of seven luminaries. I think the only people who didn't enjoy it as much were the commentators themselves. They are used to being on every 60 minutes or so, remaining in the flow of the match. In this telecast, some of them were on once in the entire session and they felt a little out of rhythm.

A day before the match began, the phone in my hotel suite was ringing constantly with ticket requests from all and sundry. It was more than unbelievable. I must have received 25 calls in three days from one high school classmate (who had played on the same cricket team as me) alone! The hotel staff would knock on my door to bring in fresh fruit every half-hour (usually they do it once a day) and to politely ask if I could spare a ticket. I must have bought over 200 tickets and then given them away. I wished I had more.

My sister Jeanne, who was by my side the whole time, assisting me in my efforts, suggested that this would be the right time to throw a party. Despite the tensions in preparing for the match, a big bash was organised at the poolside of the Taj West End Hotel.

It was a wonderful prelude to the great cricket action the next day. Imran, Ifty and his wife Sameena flew in specially from Pakistan, Parmesh and Adi Godrej made it from Bombay, Star TV's Andrew Carnegie and Gene Swinstead joined Sunil Gavaskar and Ravi Shastri. Jagoo Dalmiya, the man who was instrumental in bringing the World Cup to the subcontinent and convenor of PILCOM came that evening, as did ICC Chairman Sir Clyde Walcott, Vijay Mallya, the Indian and Pakistan cricket teams and a host of my friends and family.

Even in this relaxed setting, you could sense the tension in the air when talking to the players who would take the field the next day. This match was to be a case of 'winner takes all' and every player was well aware of the pressures of the situation.

The next morning, I watched some of the other quarter-finals being played that day, between Sri Lanka and England, and then drove off to the cricket stadium with Imran and Jonathan

Bottom: *From left to right, first row: Kerry Sweeney, Sohrab Boga, Viv Greig, Jeanne Boga, Tony Greig, second row: Sue Reef, Karen Mascarenhas, Mark Mascarenhas, Borys Mascarenhas, Gene Swinstead, Parmesh Godrej and Vijay Mallya.*

Mermagen. Imran told me that I looked nervous, and we joked apprehensively about what was to come.

When we arrived at the ground, the Indian team was practising hard. Imran was surprised that they had taken to the field so early. He told me that in his days as Captain of Pakistan, he would bring his squad to the ground only a few minutes before they were required to do so. According to him, this ensured that the players didn't have time to start thinking too much before the game began, didn't have time to get nervous.

Despite all the hype and build-up, the match lived up to all of our expectations. Sidhu and Tendulkar got the Indian side off to a flying start with some excellent batting, and then the remaining four lead order batsman added solid contributions to put the finishing touches on the innings.

Imtiaz Ahmed, whom I played for when he was my school captain, and who went on to play first-class cricket, was the local official assigned to help me at the stadium. He was exceptionally kind and attentive and there was a constant flow of refreshments throughout the match. During overs or a drink break, he would accompany the bearer and I'd ask my old skipper for his opinion on the match. He insisted everything was fine and India had wickets in hand but neither he nor anyone else could have predicted that Jadeja was going to slaughter Waqar Younis's bowling.

We spent the interval at the WorldTel hospitality centre in the clubhouse. Everyone seemed confident that India had accumulated enough runs to see the side through to victory.

Then Sohail and Anwar started to take the Indian bowling attack apart with some devastating offensive batting. All of India held its breath. Wickets fell at regular intervals, but

there was no collapse except that every time one fell, the run rate would decrease from the phenomenal start by Pakistan's openers. When Latif and Miandad were at the wicket, it seemed as though the match was touch-and-go, but with the huge, wildly enthusiastic crowd behind them India continued to get the breaks they needed at the time they needed them most.

When the match ended after the 49th over, the stadium erupted. I had never seen anything like this before. The players had returned to the front of the pavillion for the Man of the Match ceremony, and I stepped on the ground to congratulate them.

When I saw Azhar he opened his arms and we hugged each other in delight. I had seen him captain India against Pakistan three times in the last two years and India had lost twice, the other encounter was rained out in Colombo. I didn't realise it then but our embrace was carried live across the world accompanied by Greigy's expert commentary.

It was a tremendous hard fought victory that reverberated across the subcontinent.

After the game, all of us got together in my hotel suite, Imran joined us — later in this book you will read about his despondency over the results. But this was the very first time in my relationship with Imran, dating back to 1993 when we first started working together on cricket telecasts, that India had beaten Pakistan. In fact, the victory for India was the first over Pakistan in a long time. The last one had been a full four years ago at the last World Cup in Australia.

Later that evening, Ijaz and Wasim Akram came to my suite to meet Imran. While I felt a little sad for Wasim because he is such a great guy as well as one of the world's most devastating fast bowlers, and Pakistan had missed him on the field because of his injury, nothing could take away from the sheer joy of that famous Indian victory. The tumultuous celebrations that swept the Garden City that night will remain with me for the rest of my life.

The consensus emerged among my expert commentators (with the notable exception of Greigy) that India was now surely on its way to the final and possibly another World Cup title.

We arrived for the semi-final (India vs Sri Lanka) in Calcutta to find the entire city had been gripped by cricket fever. The Eden Gardens provided an awesome backdrop for yet another gripping match as the home team battled it out against everyone's favourite underdog. India won the toss and elected to field.

The WorldTel team was sitting in the first two rows of the upper deck of the B.C. Roy club house, which was equipped with a television monitor. I was joined by Viv Greig and

Andrew Carnegie. When the Indian bowlers struck to take two Sri Lankan wickets in the first over, Carnegie almost went over the railing!

But the Sri Lankans fought back against the odds as they had since the tournament began. Aravinda de Silva played what I thought was the knock of the World Cup, laying the foundation for his team's match-winning total.

Sri Lanka had soundly beaten the home side on their own turf.

Mick Jagger happened to be at the Eden Gardens for the match and I had invited him up to the commentary box where he enjoyed himself talking to the commentary crew. Later that evening, he joined us in my hotel suite. Seeing the look of disappointment and sadness on my face Mick said 'Mark, you must learn from us Englishmen, we are fully experienced in coping with losing.' The whole room burst into laughter. But when we left the next day for Chandigarh by chartered aircraft, the mood was still quite sombre. India would take some time to recover from the loss that ended their team's World Cup run.

Chandigarh:

The facilities at Mohali were impressive, Inder's wife Kamal and her team of volunteers had done a great job of preparing the clubhouse. Vijay Mallya was there with his United Breweries team to watch the West Indies which was sponsored by one of his beer brands, Kingfisher.

Top: **From left to right, Borys Mascarenhas, Andrew Carnegie, Tony Greig, Mark Mascarenhas, Inder Bindra, Vijay Rekhi and S. Gupte.**

Bottom: **A dejected Richie Richardson congratulates the victorious Aussies.**

When four Australian wickets fell quickly, and with both of the dynamic Waugh brothers back in the pavillion, Vijay and I were in the West Indies dressing-room with Wesley Hall and Andy Roberts. Vijay was ecstatic, so thrilled that he made the rest of us feel as though we were on top of the moon even though there was still plenty of cricket to play.

As the West Indies innings developed, it looked as though Lara and Chanderpaul had taken their team into the clear winning position. But then Shane Warne struck, and the West Indies wound up 'snatching defeat from the jaws of victory.'

Lahore:
Our final stop in a journey that had crisscrossed three countries and hundreds of thousands of miles. The city was to provide us with unforgettable experiences.

On my first night there, Javed Miandad came to our hotel and took all of us — Tony, Viv, Ian, Ravi, Geoffrey and myself — to visit his palatial home. It was my first time, meeting Javed in person.

Was he ever entertaining! He told us story after story, the most impressive to me being the exact account of how he hit Chetan Sharma's last ball for a six to beat India at Sharjah, a stroke that devastated millions of Indian fans.

The next day brought more great experiences. Imran's good friend Yusuf Salaludin invited us all to his magnificent home in the centre of downtown Lahore. It reminded me of a beautiful palazzo in southern Italy. Mick was there with his daughter Jade and many of Imran's friends from England. Later on, Nusrat Fateh Ali Khan sang. On our way back to the hotel we stopped at Salman and Amna Taseer's party, where another 300 guests were dining and dancing. It was all very festive.

QUALITY, CHOICE & GOOD VALU[E]
ONLY AT PACE

The Lahore stadium was very impressive, as was the stadium in Karachi. They had undergone extensive renovations. I found the architect's designs appealing and the quality of construction appeared to be very good. The construction work at these venues were arguably the best I've ever seen in the subcontinent.

But we still didn't know what was in store for us at the stadium on the day of the final...

During the course of the World Cup, I had been given the allocated tickets by PILCOM to every match. But when my staff asked Arif Abbasi, in Lahore, about the tickets we were politely informed that there were none! Meanwhile, the premium ticket stands next to the pavillion were in complete chaos. People without tickets had occupied seats and were refusing to move from them. It was clear that the management, which had been organised through a foreign company, left a lot to be desired. After all, local officials who have full knowledge of the situation on the ground would never have allowed this embarrassing chaos to take place. One of the many victims was Arun Poorie who had come all the way from New Delhi, and had to retreat to his hotel to watch the game. We had to start a mad scramble to find seats and our group was split up.

When I got into the venue with my credential from Calcutta, I ran into Imran in the pavillion. He heard my account of our predicament and replied, 'What about me Mark. I brought the last World Cup home to Pakistan, I have the best record as the captain of Pakistan, played for my country for twenty years and still have not been given a ticket or invitation to the match.'

Finally, I ended up with headphones and a monitor alone at the back of the third umpire's box. If John Reid had had his way, I'd have been out. Clive Lloyd, the match referee who was present in the box, saved the day for me. He whispered something quietly in John's ear and then John started to become progressively more tolerant of my presence. By the interval he seemed quite happy with me and later came over to apologise for his earlier remarks.

And then Sri Lanka emerged as the heroes of the tournament. Starting off by being rebuffed by the West Indies and Australian cricket teams who refused to play in their country, the 'third wheel' of cricket in the subcontinent had made it all the way to the Cup finals against the odds. After their triumph over India at the Eden Gardens, I was rooting for them as I had been involved with broadcasting their matches, starting with the 1994 Singer World Series in Colombo.

In October 1995, less than a year before the World Cup final, Sri Lanka had won its first one-day international tournament in Sharjah, with impressive victories over Pakistan and the West Indies. That tournament was also televised by WorldTel.

Besides, Australia had already won the Cup once, and if Sri Lanka could pull off an upset, it would mean that each of the three teams from the subcontinent had won the cup. Perhaps most importantly, in addition to their excellence on the field, most observers in the cricket world would agree that the Sri Lanka side consists of the most unassuming and warm-hearted group of individuals playing the game today.

I have to give Greigy credit. He spotted them early, stayed with Sri Lanka as his favourites, and his prediction came true in a big way. Right before the quarter-finals, Simon Reed called me from London to say that he had just bet on Sri Lanka to win the cup at 33-1odds. In retrospect, I wish I had joined him in his wager.

As the World Cup developed, Sachin Tendulkar, Shane Warne and Mark Waugh did a great job for their teams and for our telecasts, with brilliant performances with the bat and ball, and in the field.

But in the end, it was that most charming and affable stroke player, Aravinda de Silva who delivered the goods for his team.

Aravinda's performance, combined with Arjuna Ranatunga's experience and leadership, propelled Sri Lanka to victory. Their inspirational journey led them to become only the fifth team in history, after the West Indies, India, Australia and Pakistan, to wear the title — Cricket World Cup Champions.

Now that the World Cup was over, I was looking forward to sitting back and relaxing!

My wife Karen and I were guests of Parmesh and Adi Godrej at a party they were throwing at their beautiful home in Juhu for the Crown Prince and Princess of Yugoslavia. Karen and I stayed there along with Mark Shand, Jonathan Mermagen and his girlfriend Nadine. Unfortunately, while the rest of the party were enjoying themselves on the beach and in the pool, I was sitting inside, on the phone with a customs officer in Calcutta, trying to get him to release our World Cup equipment.

The reason he claimed for the detention of the equipment was that Doordarshan had not paid a duty of $250,000 from a year ago. He would not accept that WorldTel was not Doordarshan and that the World Cup equipment was WorldTel's. He wouldn't listen to reason, nor would he accept a guarantee from the Information and Broadcasting Ministry. The overrun costs were mounting and I decided that I had to pay it.

At the time of writing, we have yet to be reimbursed.

After this customs fiasco, I walked away feeling that something must be done soon about deregulating television in India.

Doordarshan is a gold mine, but its entire structure needs overhauling. The powers that be seem to fear that if television falls into private hands it may not serve the public interest, so they retain all the reins of power and exercise this power in a parochial manner. In my opinion, this feudal system definitely does not serve the public interest.

In a proper democracy, it is hard for big institutions to fall in the wrong hands, especially when you have a public body as a watchdog. This system already works in the financial arena for the average Indian investing in companies like Tata's and Reliance. Why can't the Indian government auction off frequencies to Indian powerhouses instead of allowing foreigners to conquer the country via satellite?

Why can't the politicians in New Delhi allow distinguished citizens like Soli Sorabjee, Charles Correa, Ratan Tata, Iqbal Chagla, Girish Karnad and Mike Khanna to sit on a television watchdog committee protecting the interests of the nation as the television network owned by the Ambanis competes with one owned by Godrej?

Imran Khan

The World Cup was disappointing in one way, in that it didn't really start until the quarter finals. The early rounds were basically practice matches, of no great interest to anyone; there never was much doubt about who would be in the quarter finals, even when Australia and the West Indies forfeited their games in Sri Lanka. In that way it was a little bit of a let-down. But once the quarter-final stage started, it became very interesting indeed, a very high-pressure competition. The knockout element makes the game dynamic — the sudden kill gives it an entirely different complexion, and it's the players who play well under pressure who come through.

And in this context I have to say that Sri Lanka did very well. At first I thought they had such an easy run, with the concessions by Australia and the West Indies at the beginning. And then they just brushed England aside in the quarter-final. It reminded me of the way Pakistan steamed through to the semi-final in 1987 without being tested. And then when we were tested, we collapsed. But Sri Lanka didn't look back. It was very impressive.

One of the things people didn't seem to notice at the time was that Sri Lanka were probably the most experienced team in the competition, especially in the batting, both in terms of years and in terms of one-day experience. And when it came down to the last two matches they were absolutely at their best; they took the pressure really well, and rose to the occasion. Most important of all, they became a team that could adapt — they could chase and win, or they could bat first and win. Their bowling was not perhaps world class, but it was ideally suited to pitches that take spin. And the way they destroyed England — it was a mismatch, really. England looked like a pedestrian team; you wouldn't have thought that eighteen counties could produce such a poor performance. But that's another story.

Of course the big plus for Sri Lanka, which everyone remarked on, was Jayasuriya. I remember he made his debut against us in 1990, and you could see then that he had a great eye and played sweet shots. Even during the World Cup people looked at him and thought he was riding his luck. But he'd played a hundred or so one-day internationals, so he knew exactly what he was doing.

So Sri Lanka were excellent. And it is true that they turned on its head my strategy in the previous World Cup, which was to start slowly and accelerate at the end. But the conditions were very different in Australia. On the wickets of the subcontinent you can take chances that would be fatal on Australian pitches. And in Australia they used two new balls, which affected our strategy a great deal. We knew that we were vulnerable to the moving ball, and that's why we began slowly — we had to conserve our early wickets. People forget, but we had quite an inexperienced team. Aamir Sohail and Inzaman ul-Haq were on debut and Salim Malik was hopelessly out of form. I was injured myself when it came to bowling. But that was why I promoted myself up the order, to contain the moving ball. Sri Lanka played in a very different way, and they made it work. The main thing was, they did have a strategy. It was carefully worked out and they stuck to it. You could see that in Calcutta, when India took two wickets in the first over, Aravinda de Silva came out and batted with the same freedom as before. He got fifty in no time and they ended up winning the match.

Of course for me, personally, the big disappointment was in Bangalore, where Pakistan lost. I was commentating that day and it was a huge occasion. And Pakistan made a bad mistake over the way they handled Wasim Akram's injury. I know what he was trying do. He was trying to give his team hope that he could play, and hoping perhaps that by some miracle he would be fit. But that was never going to happen.

When I saw him suffer the injury against New Zealand I knew. I've injured just about every bone or muscle that can be injured in my 21 years of cricket, and I knew straightaway that it was a rib injury, and that it would take a minimum of three weeks. I had the same injury once, and it took me four weeks to get back — and I was young then. It really is a nasty injury.

This is with hindsight of course, but what they should have done was keep the other side guessing, not allow them the psychological advantage. But inside the team it should have been clear that Wasim wasn't going to play, so that they could plan the game properly. As it was, he pulled out at the last minute and the team was rudderless. You could see it as soon as they took the field. They had incredible field settings; they were immediately on the defensive. They didn't seem to have a game-plan at all. It was distressing to be commentating when you could see the confusion out there. And it was such an extraordinary occasion. Matches between Pakistan and India are always high pressure events, and this was the first game on Indian soil in however many years. The crowd was roaring, and it was an intimidating atmosphere. You expect that. But it was one of those days when all the players have to know exactly what is expected of them.

I was sad, obviously, when Pakistan lost. Many of the players had played in Australia in 1992, so I felt close to that team. And I have no doubt that Pakistan were the best team in the World Cup. I have no doubt about this; I've said it many times. I know that Sri Lanka played very well, but Pakistan had more talent and variety than any other team in the competition. In Australia, as I've said, we were quite inexperienced. And we didn't have Waqar Younis or Rashid Latif. Salim Malik was in much better form, Mushtaq Ahmed was at the top of his game — this was just a much stronger all-round team. And then they had this wonderful bowler, Saqlain Mushtaq.

When Pakistan lost to South Africa in Karachi I wrote that I thought it was because they were a bowler short. On the easy-paced wickets of Pakistan, it was a waste having a specialist number six batsman. How many times in one-day internationals has a number six batsman made a difference to the winning total? If the top five fail, the sixth can very rarely save the day. Anyway, against South Africa the big difference was the fifth bowler. South Africa gave the ball to young Paul Adams, and he made the difference. So the only thing I said on the morning of the match in Bangalore was that they must play this boy, Saqlain. They needed a specialist bowler instead of getting overs out of Salim Malik and Aamir Sohail in the middle. That's when they should have been keeping the pressure on. Instead, they allowed India to accumulate runs easily at four an over, and then when the slog came, well, anything can happen then. Anyone can get hit, even Waqar Younis!

And then when they batted they got the start they needed, and this is where Sri Lanka would have capitalised. But Pakistan lost their heads and in that atmosphere, as soon as wickets started falling the pressure really mounted. They should have checked themselves — of course it's easy enough to say that now, but it's in these pressure situations that you have to perform if you want to win.

Commentating on that match was difficult, because I very much wanted Pakistan to win. I would have loved them to have won. And commentating for me is like a holiday. It couldn't be a profession for me. Politically it was interesting in Pakistan because the government tried so hard to capitalise on the cricket team. They spent lots of money And it was a pity, really, because the government was so unpopular — you could feel that in Lahore when Benazir arrived at the ground and everyone booed. But the government was determined to make political capital out of the World Cup. There was so much hype, and in all the excitement they forgot that we could lose; they never catered for losing. So it backfired on the government quite badly when we did lose.

It has been said that the World Cup didn't really work as a spectator event in Pakistan, but the people are not stupid; they knew the early matches were not significant. And it's true that hardly anyone went to the quarter final between England and Sri Lanka, but that's because it was on the same day as the match between India and Pakistan. Perhaps what this showed, above all, is the importance of television in the modern game. People preferred to watch the game on television rather than go to the ground. Television didn't really make a big impact until the late 1980s, but there's no doubt it has had a transforming effect. It's taken the game into remote areas, spread cricket across the country in an unprecedented way. I'm feeling the effects of that in a new way now.

Through cricket, my name has travelled everywhere in Pakistan. So when people say that hardly anyone went to the matches, they're wrong if they think that means that Pakistan doesn't love cricket. It's just that television is the new force in the game. That's where people watch cricket now.

Ian Chappell

The 1996 World Cup was a great boost to cricket, in addition to being a wonderful advertisement for the one-day game.

The format of twelve teams worked, despite criticism from the anti-expansionists. Anyone who witnessed the players from Holland valiantly striving to save runs at the lovely Baroda ground, couldn't help but be impressed by the endeavour of the Dutchmen. Then the Kenyans provided the ultimate slap in the face for critics of the extended format by comprehensively beating the once mighty West Indies in their group A contest.

Having been impressed by the skill of young players like Steve Tikolo, Maurice Odumbe and Kennedy Otieno, it's not a case of having an overactive imagination to visualise the next new force in the World Cup. It took Sri Lanka only twenty-one years to rise from obscurity to world champions and by casting the mind forward to 2017 it's possible to see a time when Kenya will be an extremely competitive side.

However, the most impressive aspect of the 1996 World Cup was the way the captains varied their tactics. By allowing their imagination to roam free they unleashed the one-day game from the encumbrance of being tagged a heavily formatted brand of cricket. Following the innovative examples set by Arjuna Ranatunga and Mark Taylor, no one can be in any doubt who is to blame if in future the game becomes stereotyped. Administrators take note; the laws don't need constant tinkering, but it doesn't hurt to deliver the occasional sharp reminder to captains that they have a duty to the patrons, the television audience and the game.

Sir Donald Bradman once said about cricketers, 'We are all custodians of the game.' That being true, Ranatunga and Taylor showed themselves to be two of the more adventurous trustees and the game owes them a debt of gratitude.

By courtesy of their innovative ploys and aggressive approach the world began to look at the one-day game in a different light. 'Traditionalists' should no longer view the abbreviated version of the game as an upstart relation whose sole purpose is to bring in money, while in the process lowering the tone of the game. It should now be seen for what it is: an entertaining brand of cricket, different from the longer version, but of equal importance in all aspects.

The new World Cup champions must take a lot of credit for this occurrence. They provided great entertainment culminating in a third World Cup Final century when Aravinda de Silva tailored a hundred that is fit to rank with the earlier efforts of Clive Lloyd and Viv Richards. However, the Sri Lankans made their intentions clear long before the final. From the moment Sanath Jayasuriya and Romesh Kaluwitharana launched a daring raid on the Indian new-ball bowlers at Delhi, the Sri Lankans had cast the die and other teams realised it was a matter of adapt or be buried under an avalanche of runs. Ranatunga's rampaging run getters caused a number of captains to don their thinking cap before putting on a protective helmet.

Taylor wasn't far behind Ranatunga in his desire to be innovative. His main tool of aggression was Shane Warne, whom he used regularly as a stock bowler and occasionally as a pinch-hitter, but Taylor also cleverly utilised Michael Bevan's wrist spin at critical moments. The West Indies, South Africa and even staid old England attempted to beef up their challenge by using hitters at the top of the order. In addition, Pakistan harassed opponents with two dashers in Aamir Sohail and Saeed Anwar who are every bit as destructive as their Sri Lankan counterparts.

The previously spin-shy South Africans signalled they were caught up in the mood. Skipper Hansie Cronje showed himself to be adaptable by using unorthodox spinner Paul Adams judiciously and the Republic's batsmen totally confused Pakistan leg-spinner Mushtaq Ahmed by sweeping virtually all his offerings. It was a joy to watch such tactical jousting, which produced enthralling cricket as well as some nail-biting contests.

The 1996 World Cup also provided curators with some food for thought. Dry, third day pitches that didn't hamper batsmen, but offered incentive for the wiles of the good spinner, didn't do the one-day game any harm.

The successful 1996 World Cup has given the game a mandate to step boldly into the new century by continuing to spread its wings. The 1998 Commonwealth Games in Kuala Lumpur will provide another platform for innovative thinking, while the programme for the World Cup in South Africa in 2004 should include matches in both Zimbabwe and Kenya.

The spread of the game has been quickened by improved and extended television coverage and WorldTel played its part in this process by successfully showcasing the World Cup.

While cricket officials talked about 'chaotic' travel arrangements for the teams, the television schedule worked well. Sure, there was the odd hitch as you would expect in a massive coverage spread over three countries, involving millions of dollars of equipment being transported thousands of miles, but the coverage was good. Despite travelling by air, rail and road there was always a car at the airport to meet the commentators and (with one notable exception in Vizag) they made the grounds on time. For that we can thank the tireless workers from Grand Slam who performed their tasks well and retained their sense of humour.

However, the man who deserves the credit for having the vision and the courage to gamble in the first place is Mark Mascarenhas of WorldTel.

Mark's success in bringing top class coverage to the subcontinent was important for both the people of the region and the game. Mascarenhas' success means that cricket now has another alternative in televising the game. Where in the past it had been up to the BBC, Channel Nine or TWI to cover cricket adequately, suddenly there was a good new player, in the region of cricket's greatest popularity.

The fact that Mascarenhas pulled it all together and kept the coverage at an acceptable standard was a credit to his vision and energy. Mark reminded me a lot of Kerry Packer in the early days of World Series Cricket (WSC). Mark is a

big man like Kerry and both had a dream they followed closely, adopting a hands-on approach.

One small gesture explains the importance of Mark's success to the region. At a dinner in Lahore at Javed Miandad's house, the effusive Pakistani walked up and hugged Mascarenhas, saying, 'Our Mark. You've done it.'

'Our Mark.' When I heard those words uttered by a Pakistani about an Indian, I realised the World Cup coverage had been a success.

||||

Top: **E.A.S. Prasanna, considered by Chappell to be the greatest spinner he faced with Shane Warne.**

Tony Greig

Presenting the 1996 World Cup telecast for Mark Mascarenhas' WorldTel was great fun and a wonderful experience. For quite some time I've been looking forward to getting back to India, Pakistan and Sri Lanka because during my cricket career I'd come to love these countries and their inhabitants and have always been fascinated by the great passion they all have for the game.

Touring this part of the world as a Test cricketer is a different experience in so much as one very soon finds out what it's really like to be an entertainer. During my playing days, cricket grounds, full to the rafters everywhere we went, filled me with the injection of enthusiasm sometimes required after the boredom associated with empty grounds and the lethargic attitude relevant in County Cricket Committee rooms and amongst many of the cricketers in England.

To be invited to be part of the 1996 World Cup broadcast provided me and my fellow commentators with the opportunity to expose to the cricket world what can only be described as an incredible suncontinental sporting experience.

It takes a slightly different kind of frame of mind to enjoy the subcontinent to the full. There is absolutely no point in being in too much of a hurry because circumstances will slow you down. Bad tempers are exposed for what they are. Traffic and most airports are chaotic and yet adventurous. The top hotels are superb, while gently easing into the local food will, given time, result in regular cravings for their culinary delights.

I don't think I experienced a spicy meal until I was in my late teens but now I am an addict. It's a big mistake to stick with Western-style menus. During the World Cup, the chilli crabs I devoured in Bombay were as good a meal as I have eaten

anywhere, while dinner at Javed Miandad's place in Lahore was as good as it gets.

The 1996 World Cup will be remembered for the incredible performance of the 'little' Sri Lankans. They took the limited overs game by the throat by introducing a tactic not previously used at international level. They attacked wildly during the initial 15 overs. My guess is that their strategy was not plotted in a moment of wisdom by a group of gurus — it evolved from the talent available in this team. Romesh Kaluwitharana and Sanath Jayasuriya were always going to be real go-getters while Aravinda de Silva and Arjuna Ranatunga were always going to accumulate. Add to these four, seven other highly talented cricketers in their own right and the winning formula was partially there. Furthermore, the confidence they found in Australia after their very tough tour to that part of the world just prior to the World Cup

Tony Greig

campaign hardened even the normally fragile members of their squad.

Leadership is always a factor during a tough competition and Arjuna, Aravinda, Dave Watmore and Duleep Mendis deserve special mention. To keep this team focused during the period leading up to the Cup, especially in Australia where they were accused of cheating and had to live through the Muthiah Muralitharan chucking debacle was a credit to all of them and the Sri Lankan Board members.

While the refusal of Australia and the West Indies to visit Sri Lanka for their preliminary matches was in my view an overreaction, lacking in understanding and foresight, it had little effect on the Cup except to create a rift between Australia and India in particular. This hopefully will heal sooner rather than later because Australia, India and South Africa are the most innovative of the cricketing nations and any ongoing rift or petty jealousies will hinder cricket's development worldwide at a time when the very opposite is required.

There were those who knocked the opening ceremony but for me that is the subcontinent. Perfection in this neck of the woods has to be measured by local standards not by those of foreign journalists and the like. For me the occasion, the passion for the game, the unbelievable excitement of the local fans was far more important than the entertainment or the facilities. From a commentary point of view it was an experience that I for one will never forget.

Just to watch India play Pakistan was fantastic. The build up, the speculation, the roar of the crowd, and at the end of the day the jubilation and of course the disappointment had to be experienced firsthand if one is to understand the passion associated with these contests.

The Australian miracle of Chandigarh was one of the best games I have ever watched and to see the 'little' Sri Lankans pull it off in Lahore was simply a pleasure.

The logistical nightmare associated with moving hundreds of people and all the television equipment from venue to venue, sometimes with very limited time available, was a credit not only to WorldTel and Grand Slam but to everyone involved in the telecast. Many people forget that years of hard work go into the preparation associated with bringing big events to the homes of millions around the world.

In the end though, we will remember this tournament as the one Sri Lanka won. Rank outsiders at the start but convincing champions in the end.

Thanks India, thanks Pakistan and thanks Sri Lanka — we loved every minute of it!

Sunil Gavaskar

Legend has it that the 1987 World Cup came to India because the President of the Indian Cricket Board in 1983, Mr. N.K.P. Salve, was given only two complimentary tickets for the finals of the 1983 World Cup. The legend further goes that so incensed was Mr. Salve at being given only two tickets (for himself and his wife) that he vowed to have the next World Cup in India if India won the event. Now on the morning of the finals or till a good one hour after the West Indies commenced their chase of the Indian total, it looked as if Mr. Salve's vow would be stillborn. But cricket is a funny game and, lo and behold, India went on to defeat the mighty West Indies and won the World Cup.

Now came the tricky part, for the previous World Cups were held in England and nobody, absolutely nobody, had dared question why a World Cup should be held in only one country. Have you heard of soccer World Cups or for that matter, the Olympics, being held in only one country? So, as soon as India (with Pakistan as co-host), bid for the 1987 World Cup, there was consternation in the country not bigger than the state of Maharashtra (in India) as to how anybody could dare to take the World Cup away from them. Wasn't cricket ruled by them and were they not the only ones who knew what was good for the game? And would those natives in the subcontinent who were constantly sniping at each other be able to organise such a huge event which would involve crisscross travelling from one country to another?

But then the subcontinent not only offered more participation money to the respective Boards but also more prize money than the measly sums that were on offer for the previous World Cups. Why, the Indian Board gave much more to the players that won the World Cup than the prize money they got for winning it!

Anyway much to the chagrin and disappointment of the doubters, the 1987 World Cup went off smoothly excepting of course the fact that England did not win it. For a country no bigger than the State of Maharashtra to *not* win the World Cup was obviously some sort of a fix by the natives in the subcontinent and imagine losing the finals to the people they once banished to a land called Australia years and years ago.

Just think... all this would not have happened if Mr. Salve had been given some more tickets.

Much the same thing happened in 1992. This was after the World Cup in Australia which, by the way, had no increase in appearance money or prize money from 1987, but then cricket is immune to inflation and market forces which is not surprising really. After all, how much can you see when your head is buried in the sands? So when the bid for the next World Cup came in, India and Pakistan along with Sri Lanka, put in an offer which was much more than Old Blighty and had them sputtering in their gin and tonics.

Mind you, as in the previous World Cup in 1987, all the sponsorship and legwork was to be done by India. Pakistan and Sri Lanka were there only for their votes and when the Associate members found that three of them could qualify for the World Cup they also decided that they would have the World Cup in the subcontinent rather than in a country not bigger than the State of Maharashtra which did not really want them to participate and which had done nothing to develop their cricket.

So all kinds of accusations of chicanery and bribing made the rounds in the papers of a country not bigger than the State of Maharashtra, but what these self-righteous people forgot was that the world is driven by commerce today and

not a bit of sentiment. By showing no awareness of commerce and no sentiment towards the struggling Associate Member countries, their chances were virtually nil.

What they could not fathom and, dare I say, stomach, was the market savvy and enterprise of the natives. How could people from the Third World be better aware of market forces than people from between the Second and Third world?

So the World Cup took place, but before that there was drama as the Australians and the West Indies pulled out of the Sri Lanka leg of the tournament because they were worried about their security after a bomb blew up in Colombo a couple of weeks before the tournament started. The Australians had just had a heated series with Sri Lanka and were worried that their players would have been targets of the terrorists but they were wrong. The target would have been the Australian umpires and not the players. The West Indies pulled out because for years they have been doing the bidding of the English and the Australians.

The tournament thus got off to just the controversial start that the media of a country not bigger than the State of Maharashtra wanted. Sure enough, their own team went out of the tournament along with the Associate Member countries and now that the men were separated from the boys, the tournament took off. The players put in inspired performances and the crowds turned up in huge numbers to watch and appreciate the game. There was disappointment for the crowds in Calcutta when their favourite players failed to perform, and that disappointment gave way to disturbances which stopped play, but apart from that it was scintillating stuff and the cricket played was top class.

But then the early exit of a country not bigger than the State of Maharashtra might have had something to do with the high quality of cricket seen.

TV coverage meant that the event was seen all over the world and the coverage itself was top class what with super-slow-motion cameras catching every little bit of action. There were heroes on the field but not many know the contribution of those who worked behind the scenes. The administrators, the TV crew who had a herculean job getting the equipment put up, de-rigged and then travelling on a cargo plane to the next destination. They were the ones whose untiring efforts ensured that the world could see what a success the 1996 World Cup was.

It was bigger and better than any previous World Cups and when a country small in size but with a people with big hearts won the World Cup it was truly the icing on a delicious cake!

Ravi Shastri

The 1996 World Cup, played in the Indian subcontinent in early 1996 was to my mind easily the most exciting in the tournament's 20-year history. There were 12 teams in the fray, the format was different and more challenging than before, and the result was a vindication of the glorious uncertainties of this marvellous sport.

Sri Lanka's triumph must rank as one of the greatest achievements in modern cricket. They were not only rank outsiders, but also had the mortification of facing a boycott from Australia and the West Indies, who refused to play in the lovely island country for wholly spurious reasons.

While security and player welfare are important concerns, I think the Aussies and the West Indians carried their apprehension too far. The boycott was unjustified, and left a bitter taste in the mouth of cricket lovers in the Indian subcontinent, especially in Sri Lanka, where cricket is both joy and passion. But there was one positive outcome of this ban — it inspired the Sri Lankans to sudden and dramatic cricketing excellence.

Riled by what they perceived as a damning insult to their nation, the Sri Lankans played with rare grit and inventiveness. The batting employed two pinch-hitters as openers, and both Sanath Jayasuriya and Romesh Kaluwitharana completely redefined one-day batting strategy, especially in the first 15 overs. They aimed to get 100 runs and more, and if they reached this objective the match was as good as gone for the opposition.

If they failed, there was more trouble. Aravinda de Silva was the most outstanding batsman of the tournament, and his innings in the semi-final and final (a half century on a wearing track and an unbeaten hundred to break the Australian stranglehold) were tour-de-forces. He played with gumption,

aggression and imagination, pushing into the shade batsmen of the calibre and class of Sachin Tendulkar, Brian Lara and Mark Waugh.

De Silva became the lynchpin of a batting line-up which, apart from the dynamic openers and himself, included the powerful Asanka Gurusinghe, the dainty, wristy Roshan Mahanama and the canny and resourceful Arjuna Ranatunga.

This was easily the best batting order in the competition — in terms of ability and consistency — and the spectacular performances in the semi-final and final proved this amply. The Sri Lankans built up a daring strategy of unbridled aggression in their batting, and stuck to this without fear even if they suffered early setbacks. Ultimately, this derring-do paid rich dividends.

The Sri Lankan bowling and fielding too was of a very high order, and given such all round brilliance, they certainly proved themselves to be a couple of notches above the other teams. Only two other sides in the tournament — South Africa and Australia — could match them for consistency. But South Africa, after looking invincible, were undone by the dazzling blade of Brian Lara who found his form belatedly, while Australia earned a heart-stopping victory over the West Indies but later were bled to defeat by the rampaging De Silva and Ranatunga in the final.

India and Pakistan, expected to exploit the home conditions to their advantage, flattered to deceive. India rode strongly on the shoulders of Sachin Tendulkar's dynamic batting, but after scoring a memorable victory over Pakistan in the quarter-finals ran out of steam and ideas. In the semi-final at the Eden Gardens, they were dismal.

Pakistan, unsettled by unseemly controversies within the team, nevertheless managed to hold their own till the quarter-final where they were undone by Indian adrenaline. Poor Wasim Akram, saddled with a side that had some rusty old timers and crusty newcomers, was finally left to face the ire and vitriol of his countrymen.

Most of the other sides played nondescript cricket, including the West Indies, for whom Brian Lara sparkled only intermittently. The outstanding West Indies performer was Curtly Ambrose who made light of the slow, unhopeful tracks and bowled with venom and thrust. But more than wickets, the West Indies needed runs, and these they got only in meagre quantity. Richie Richardson had a torrid time, as captain and batsman, and with Lara finding his touch only belatedly the once mighty side was reduced to the status of also-ran.

England, fatigued after a long and arduous tour of South Africa, were hopelessly exposed. They had neither the energy nor the imagination to play such a demanding tournament and simply went through the motions. New Zealand, bereft of genuine class what with Martin Crowe not being in their midst, worked in fits and starts but to no tangible benefit save providing some youngsters an opportunity to play at the highest level.

In this context, the newer teams like UAE and Kenya profited enormously by being exposed to the best cricketing talent in the world. Indeed, Kenya pulled off the upset of the tournament with a stunning victory over the West Indies and in the process revealed some exciting young players. The success of this World Cup was not restricted only to the cricket field. State-of-the-art television coverage made it the most exciting sports spectacle ever for millions of cricket fans all over the world. Slow motion replays, stump vision, spin vision and other innovations brought the viewer closer to the action than ever before. Coupled with this was the articulate, insightful and profusely entertaining commentary by a Dream Team of commentators.

Some of the members of this side were Richie Benaud, Tony Greig, Ian Chappell, Mike Holding, Sunil Gavaskar and Imran Khan. For me, to be a part of this line-up was both an honour and an education.

Ranjit Fernando

What more emotional a scene than when players, whatever the sport may be, stand to attention with clenched fists against their hearts, tears rolling down their cheeks, and sing their National Anthem with great fervour before a packed stand of countrymen in a World Cup Final. I, for years, dreamt in vain of the day when we Sri Lankans would savour such an experience.

When Arjuna and his team stood before a full house, and hundreds of millions of T.V. viewers the world over, and rendered the beautiful 'Namo Namo Matha' it was a dream come true for every Sri Lankan who felt a part of this memorable moment.

Hair on end, I stood in the television commentary box, honoured to be in the company of Richie Benaud, Tony Greig, Ian Chappell, Sunil Gavaskar, Geoff Boycott and Ravi Shastri, some of the greatest names the cricketing world has known. The wetness around my eyes and the lump in my throat did not deter me joining the singing, as I was not going to deny myself this wonderful sensation for anything in this world.

This was only the end of the beginning. The paradise island of Sri Lanka was agog with excitement. The shop shutters went up, and the roads were deserted except for the lively gatherings around T.V. sets at street corners. There was a small party in virtually every Sri Lankan home with lion flags of all sizes being waived proudly before television sets.

Our team was out there battling against the might of Australia in the final. The popular brew 'arrack' was consumed in varying quantities and the spirits were very high well before the end of the Australian innings.

Every run was cheered with gusto and with intense patriotism when Arjuna and Aravinda clawed their way

towards the target score. It was no different the world over, wherever there were Sri Lankans.

All hell broke loose and Sri Lanka erupted when the skipper Ranatunga scored the winning runs. The World Cup was ours. Sri Lankans took to the streets in their thousands, but this time all united, hugging each other with tears of joy. Shouts of 'Jaya Weva' and the sounds of trumpets rent the air. Flags were waved and the never ending burst of crackers greeted the victory. Car horns tooted and 'Baila' was danced to the rhythms of improvised drums. The wailing of trumpets and the sound of drums became deafening as the musicians broke into a joyous frenzy as the night wore away. The carnival and merrymaking continued till the wee hours of the morning.

When Arjuna Ranatunga held the World Cup high, the scenes at the Gaddafi Stadium were just unbelievable. The Pakistan crowds went berserk as if their side had won. Mayhem prevailed with even Sri Lanka's victory lap (at the helm of which were the cheer leaders Percy and Lionel) falling into total disarray. In the safety of the dressing room, the Sri Lankan cricketers in hushed silence, with their heads bowed and palms together before their faces, gave thanks to the Almighty. They were carrying the feelings, aspirations and thanksgiving of all Sri Lankans. There were no differences of race, caste or creed. There was no question of 'I did it' or 'he did it.' 'We Sri Lankans did it together' was the theme. Players were also seen paying obeisance to their parents and elders who had been with them through thick and thin, going down on their knees and venerating them in traditional style.

The champagne popped and flowed and this popular bunch of cricketers were the toast of the cricket world. They did not want to share this glory alone and wished to go back home the same night.

Air Lanka's 'City of Anuradhapura' which brought a full complement of passengers on a special charter to watch the final was their only chance. Some of the passengers volunteered to return on a scheduled flight to send their heroes home. Around 5.00 in the morning Air Lanka flight UL 1184, skippered by former Sri Lanka cricketer Sunil Wettimuny, was homeward bound with its most precious cargo. Everyone was weary, it was a long day with little sleep, but with the champagne laid on board the party went on in grand Sri Lankan style. The singing and dancing talents of Aravinda's father Sam, and Roshan's dad Upali were on display. They led the way and were joined by all. The proud Minister of Sports, Hon. S.B. Dissanayake and some of his Cabinet colleagues were a part of the happy group. The team

arrived to a ticker-tape welcome. The crowds spontaneously lined the streets from the Katunayake airport to Colombo, a distance of around 18 miles.

Arjuna with the World Cup held aloft, walked slowly down the gangway with his victorious team trooping behind, to the mad cacophony of cheers, drums and music.

The roar from thousands lining the streets and the mighty chorus drowned the music and drumming when the motorcade swept into Colombo.

An audience with Her Excellency, The President Chandrika Bandaranaike Kumaratunga, who had closely followed the

destinies of the team, was the culmination of the motorcade.

When the public appearances were done, there was skipper Ranatunga personally visiting those that paved the way for this great achievement, with the coveted trophy. Amongst them the widow of the slain Gamini Dissanayake. In triumph and in his moment of glory, he had not forgotten them. This really epitomises the humble, grateful, simple Sri Lankan cricketers who had charmed millions and held the world spellbound. Sri Lanka had finally made an indelible mark in this fiercely competitive world of sport. Cricket had produced a new breed of sporting heroes.

Richie Benaud

I knew something was up when Wes Hall came across to us, beaming and confident at a moment when he might have been perceived to be morose and unsmiling. The West Indies had moved on to Jaipur, for their match with the Australians in the World Cup, and they were coming off a hammering by Kenya in their previous round match played at Pune. The West Indies were bowled out then for 93 and were lucky to make that many. Yet here was Wesley Winfield moving briskly across to Ian Chappell and me as we walked away from the pitch at Jaipur and giving me a finger in the chest with the words, 'we're going to beat you today, you'll see an entirely different team out there'. He was right and those two matches underlined perfectly the manner in which the game of cricket can change, no matter whether it is the five-day version or the shortened one which is finding so much favour with cricket followers around the world.

There were many reasons I so thoroughly enjoyed the World Cup, not least of which was that it was the first time I had been to India in 32 years. I retired from the international game in 1964 and since then have been overflying India on round the world trips, Australia-United Kingdom-Australia, covering cricket for television in both countries.

It is only in recent times that international cricket had taken such a television hold on the populace in India and Pakistan and the 1996 World Cup was the culmination of this. When you bear in mind that my last proper trip to India had been as captain of the Australian team on the first full-scale tour of India in 1959-60, you would imagine correctly that I saw a few changes. The most important part though was that it was a great adventure, interspersed with some brilliant and innovative cricket and some excellent and some improvised organisation.

The brilliant cricket came from many of the teams, the innovative cricket from Sri Lanka and Australia who eventually made it to the Final in Lahore. The best thing that could have happened to this tournament was that these two sides should have played in the last match, because they were not only the best teams but also were led by the best captains, Arjuna Ranatunga and Mark Taylor.

The tournament itself didn't get away to the best of starts, with the Australians and the West Indians forfeiting their matches after a Tamil Tigers' suicide bomber had killed eighty people by driving a van into the front of a building in the main shopping centre in Colombo. It was a chilling reminder of terrorism in our modern times and, understandably, there was no shortage of hype and emotion.

Four months later it was alleged that PILCOM, the organising body of the World Cup, had delayed paying Australia and West Indies their final agreed share of the World Cup guarantee. Court proceedings were mentioned as well, so perhaps all was not sweetness and light with the various administrators around the world, something which was underlined at the 1996 ICC meeting at Lord's where they failed to find some way to nominate a Chairman for the following year.

I have a suggestion for them, one which would go a long way to having them behave like a group of dedicated adults administering a multi-million dollar sport, instead of a bunch of bickering politicians. Next year, at the ICC meeting, put the names of the nine Test playing countries in a hat and draw out one marble for the country which will provide the chairman for 1998. Let's say it is Sri Lanka; they then would not be included in the draw the following year and this method, with previous chairmen's countries excluded, would continue each year. Between 1998 and 2006 the Chairmen might come, in order, from Sri Lanka, New Zealand, South

Africa, Zimbabwe, India, Pakistan, West Indies, Australia and England. The draw from the hat method would be essential so that, until 2006, political desperadoes would have no idea which country was next on the list. As far as I am concerned, the Chairman is a figurehead, though I know many cricket administrators regard it as heresy to think in that fashion about what they regard as the ultimate in life.

My view is that the power should, instead, be vested in a committee of ex-Test players and captains. Their brief would be to sort out the matters from a cricketing point of view rather than as a matter of politics!

Cricket can be a wonderful, solidifying influence around the world if it is allowed to be so. In the World Cup there was that great game of cricket between India and Pakistan in Bangalore, one of the finest matches imaginable and the players took full advantage of the rare opportunity to mix, an opportunity denied at other times because politicians are unable to agree on a variety of matters.

No better example of the extraordinary nature of the game can be found than the Australian win over the West Indies at Chandigarh. You wouldn't have wanted to put a bet of a brass razoo on Australia for most of the game. Yet, with Mark Taylor's inspirational captaincy, they drove themselves through to the Final a few days later. There the Sri Lankans were too good for them, playing some brilliant cricket, well led by Ranatunga and inspired by the classic nature of the cricket played by Aravinda de Silva. Not only did Sri Lanka win the final but they won the public relations contest as well, as they had done for some of the time in Australia where they were regarded as being cuddly and hard done by.

In fact, apart from their being innovative, they were never short of an aggressive word or two on the field and gave as good as they got and more, besides, which in my opinion is a good thing, particularly, if you manage to do it with a public relations smile for the television cameras.

For me the World Cup was a great adventure, with excellent organisation from Grand Slam and WorldTel and the tournament continued and reinforced my belief that cricket is the most controversial game of all. I just hope I'm there for the next one played in Asia.

Michael Holding

The 1996 Cricket World Cup staged in the Asian subcontinent was successful and revealing, in my view, on quite a few fronts.

Firstly, with so many sceptics around doubting the organisational skills of two countries almost at war politically, India and Pakistan along with Sri Lanka made it look, to the outside world, like a spectacle well staged with very few organisational blunders. This just proves once again that sport transcends all boundaries and obstacles placed in its way. But this World Cup also once again confirmed the influential power of the electronic media. For the millions of viewers watching their television screens around the world, the 1996 World Cup was a dream. Whatever few hiccups were encountered during the competition by those on hand (whether they be spectators, players or even the television crew themselves) the viewers at home were oblivious to these problems because when they turned on their television sets, they got just what they wanted. Nice clear pictures of their favourite teams fighting for glory.

Obviously a competition of this magnitude could not have been flawless, and the opening ceremony for one had its fair share of controversy surrounding the expense and the practicality of it all. Then of course, there was the non-participation of Australia and the West Indies in the Sri Lanka leg of the first round due to security reasons. Fortunately none of these controversies affected the competition in any real terms.

This 1996 World Cup was the biggest ever staged, in terms of participating countries, with the full quota of nine test playing countries taking part along with the first three finishers in the I.C.C. tournament staged in Kenya, a couple of years earlier. These three teams, Holland, the United Arab Emirates and Kenya made up the full complement to twelve teams divided into two zones of six teams.

Here again, the sceptics were having a field day. Before the competition even started, they were questioning the rationale of having these minnows in the competition in the first place, and pointing out the fact that the way the competition and the zones were structured they were certainly going to be amongst the first four casualties along with one other. It was also thought that the first elimination stage was too long a process to arrive at the obvious.

As the competition started and went along its merry way, the detractors' voices softened as the 'minnows' acquitted themselves well and sent a few shivers down the spines of some teams. Kenya created the shock of the tournament, choking the mighty West Indies, almost eliminating them from the competition. I must admit that the preliminary rounds did take a long time to do the obvious but it must be said in defence, that the minnows benefited greatly by playing so many games with the 'big guns' and got an ideal practical way of measuring their progress towards competing on an even footing. If this great game, cricket, is going to grow throughout the world, exposure for the minnows is

essential.Let us not forget that a few years ago, Sri Lanka were considered the beating stick of the world. The 1996 World Cup proved the world to be the beating stick of Sri Lanka.

Well, what about the tournament itself? I think the public got real value for money. Firstly, the playing conditions were ideal for limited overs cricket in that the pitches were flat to allow the bat to hold sway over the ball. Secondly, there were very few if any weather interruptions which would have necessitated the restructuring of new target scores and generally interfered with the smooth flow of the games. As stated before, there were a lot of reservations put forward by some regarding the venue of the tournament, but these were two very positive factors where limited overs cricket is concerned.

Of course with the pitches being as flat as they were, the bowlers certainly could not dominate the batsmen. The spinners had a better chance of showing off their wares than the quickies, but the batsmen really dominated proceedings. Mark Waugh, Sachin Tendulkar, Brian Lara, Aravinda de Silva and Jayasuriya stood out with some brilliant strokeplay and as we know, cricket and in particular limited overs cricket, is about balls rocketing into the sideboard and over the boundaries. At times, one almost felt sorry for the bowlers, but the flat pitches really showed who were the real stars with the ball.

The spinners, as stated before, had a better chance of being proud of what they achieved during the tournament. So Shane Warne, Mushtaq Mohammed, Pat Symcox all had their moments of glory without really dominating. But the quickies had no such luck. Allan Donald and Curtly Ambrose were the top fast bowlers who got the least punishment with Ambrose standing head and shoulders above the rest. He was the only fast bowler throughout the tournament who didn't get

hammered around the ground in any game. He, fortunately or unfortunately, depending on whether you are a West Indian backer or not, didn't get to play against Sri Lanka at all during the tournament and that surely would have been the ultimate test.

Sri Lanka definitely proved to be the most dynamic team with the bat and certainly deserve the title as World Champions of limited overs cricket. They had been shouting out to the world for a while now that they had arrived. The 1996 World Cup brought home to the rest of the world in no uncertain terms that they were not just blowing hot air.

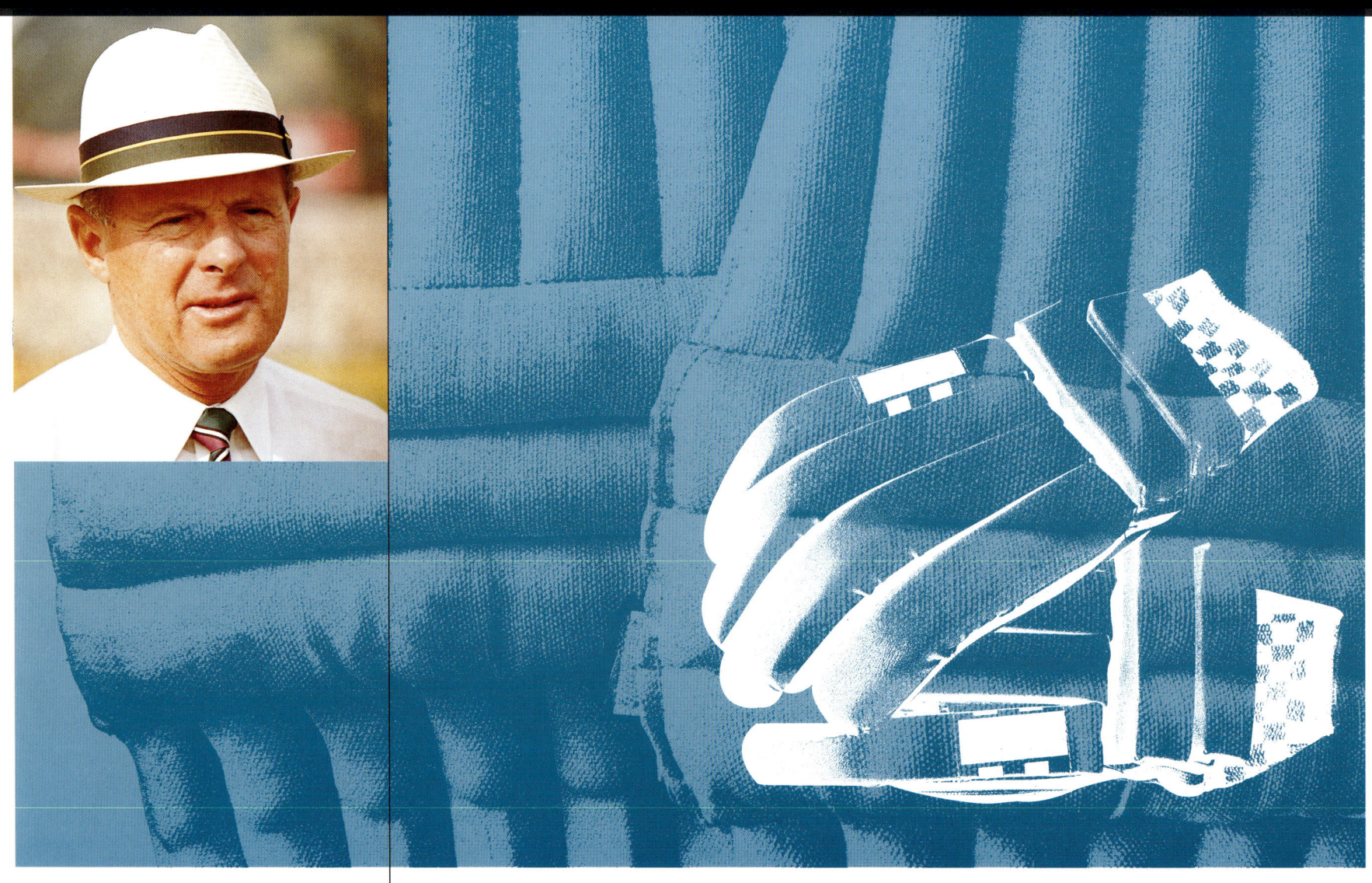

Geoffrey Boycott

For two weeks, the World Cup was a non-event. With three I.C.C. Associate teams taking part we had too many matches that were a foregone conclusion, as the minnows were no match for the main countries. Unless the home teams were playing, poor crowds meant a lack of atmosphere. So a lack of competitive element, and with few people at some of the games, this detracted from the tournament. Kenya defeating a dispirited, lack-lustre, disunited West Indies team was the shock of the tournament but it had little effect on the main teams making it to the quarter-finals when the World Cup really began.

I am all for spreading the game to more countries and giving U.A.E., Holland and Kenya an opportunity to participate in the World Cup. It is vital that all cricketers are ambitious and strive for the ultimate goal. It is good that dreams come true for some cricketers from those countries and in Kenya's case genuine distinction was earned with a historic win. But what chance did they really have against all the top countries — not a lot! If we truly want those countries to improve and eventually play the big countries on equal terms or at least play with a realistic chance of competing decently every game — not just an occasional freak win — then we must give those countries the opportunity to regularly compete with quality opposition.

In the four years leading up to the World Cup, how many times did the three I.C.C. Associate teams pit their skill against the top countries? What preparation were they given for this huge occasion?

I am so pleased that steps have been taken for Kenya to play in some South African domestic competitions, the U.A.E. in India and Holland in England's NatWest knock-out competition. It is a start but not enough. For example, Holland could and should be invited into England's Benson

and Hedges Cup and Sunday League, which would guarantee them over twenty matches per year. The same applies to Kenya and U.A.E. in South Africa and India. Players need the stimulus of lots of regular, tough, competitive cricket. The more they are stretched under pressure the better they will become.

From a personal point of view the disintegration of England was hard to behold. In recent years their Test match results haven't been great but they have always been a good one-day international side. Being losing finalists at the 1979, 1987 and 1992 World Cups supports that, and up to six months before the competition began I fancied their chances to get to the final again. Alec Stewart played the pivotal role as batsman/wicket keeper and there were plenty of dual purpose players in Chris Lewis, Philip Defreitas and Dermot Reeve.

It all changed during the tour of South Africa.

Lewis was history, Defreitas was not wanted by the captain for personal reasons and he was only called in at a late stage by the Chairman/ Manager, Ray Illingworth. Reeve was not their cup of tea as maybe the captain felt his position threatened because Reeve was the best captain in England —tactically bright, innovative and successful with Warwickshire in county cricket. If the Chairman of selectors had been far-sighted and bold, Reeve should have been made Captain for the one-day matches in South Africa and the World Cup. Robin Smith had been a match winning batsman in past one-day internationals but found his confidence sapped through innuendo from the management that he was past it; his place became dodgy. Stewart was not certain to play as batsman/wicket keeper and the pivotal role of wicket keeper was to be filled by Jack Russell. The whole balance of the team was upset with Russell in and a losing sequence

of one-dayers against South Africa just before the World Cup left the players in a poor frame of mind.

England had no settled team and were not clear on their best line-up or even their best opening batsman. Short of original ideas they were basically playing 'catch up' cricket, with a pinch-hitter, following the success of other teams. Because the captain was in poor form, he was moving up and down the order, which didn't allow the team batting order to be settled. As the tournament developed, many players were tired and it was a relief to some who were dispirited to the point that Sri Lanka won the Quarter Finals and they were off home early.

In the betting stakes to win the World Cup, Sri Lanka were not most people's choice. In recent years they had done nothing of significance with no great results and most of us

thought that they had talented stroke players but maybe a bit light on bowling and possibly not tough enough mentally when the chips were down or when under pressure. They were outsiders whom we warmed towards when Australia and West Indies wouldn't play in their country.

Sri Lanka winning the World Cup was a dream come true for the players after the distracting political beginnings. They were the newest members to Test cricket, until Zimbabwe came along, and had usually been a pushover in the big league outside of their own country. To see them play with smiles on their faces, with commitment, skill and great artistry gave every cricket lover a thrill and good feeling. It sent most of us home happy that our game could thrill and surprise us and that good things could happen to nice people. It was a fairy tale ending!

Travelogue of Ian Chappell

DELHI TOURISM
TOURIST INFORMATION AND FACILITATION

W P MORTON
ENGLAND CRICKET
TEAM

Rod Marsh can't recall it but he once told me, "adventure is discomfort remembered in tranquillity." That being the case, the television crews covering the 1996 World Cup have had one hell of an adventure.

I am writing this while flying in the Russian Ilyushin 76 aircraft that transports the TV equipment and crew around the subcontinent. The guys refer to the big kite as 'the illusion' and in this case I am trying to type while perched on top of a ton or so of television equipment, while attempting to maintain my balance as the plane shudders and moves around.

What about seat belts you ask? Not one in sight as this is a cargo plane. It also doesn't have toilets, we don't have boarding passes, or go through security and no one weighs the hand luggage, so why worry about a minor detail like being strapped in. I quite like the idea because you can actually lie down and have a sleep if you don't mind being 'woken occasionally' with a dig in the ribs from a camera case or the pointed toe of a tripod. Not so bad really, it beats a similar prod from the missus reminding me to get up and water the lawn. Actually, on second thoughts that statement is not strictly correct.

Nevertheless, these flights can rightly be called an adventure. I've made two of them, both uneventful, but the TV crew have some tales to tell.

Like the time they were taxi-ing in Delhi and there was a hell of a bang. The plane returned to the allotted parking spot on the tarmac and in the process there were two more loud explosions. On inspection it was discovered that three tyres had blown. Never mind, the full complement of twenty were made operational after a twelve hour repair job. Apparently there are twelve layers of rubber on each of the huge tyres

— better they blow while taxi-ing to take off rather than on landing.

I must say the A crew (there are four, A to D) have kept their sense of humour and continue to laugh about this adventure. Incredible really, cram about thirty people of disparate backgrounds from at least a dozen different nations in a cargo hold with a whole lot of shifting equipment and they laugh about it over a beer. Put two politicians or a couple of religious zealots in a plush airconditioned room and there's a good chance a war will result. I don't know whether that speaks volumes for beer or is an indictment of airconditioning.

Then there was the cargo door incident. The story is best told by Dave Gray of Melbourne — no, not the ugly one, th-th-this Dave stutters, says he is handsome and is actually quite funny. On the trip in question a couple of the Ukrainian flight crew engaged in a whispered conversation, then peered through the window in the door leading to the hold. One of the TV crew then decided to check for himself and discovered that the huge cargo doors weren't completely closed. Dave explained afterwards, "I w-w-wondered how come there was a shaft of light coming through the w-w-window in the airlock door."

Then there was the train, taxi, plane and bus adventure. Simple trip really, Gwalior to Vizag. About seven centimetres on a map, roughly the same length as the full name of Vishakhapatnam. Twelve hundred kilometres as the crow flies and going that way would have been a damn sight quicker. It was thirty-two hours from my arrival at the cricket ground in Gwalior to undressing in the hotel at Hyderabad, all completed without a change of gear.

The diary entries look like this. Midnight-train left Gwalior after India vs West Indies day/night. Drank beer, chatted with S. Gavaskar, Venkatapathy Raju (nickname Muscles), Prabhakar, Kumble, Mark Mascarenhas.

Sleep at 2, woken at 5 am. Sunil won't rise, so give him army wake up call; "Hands off cocks, on with socks." No effect on Sunny. Laughter from Jeanne, Mark M's sister. Name spelt same as my mother, so I do no wrong in her eyes. Sunny still

in bed so tie his shoelaces together. His hands now occupied for two hours, says he'll get even. Taxi ride at Formula One speed through streets of Delhi to make 6:30 flight to Calcutta. To relieve Richie's anxiety tell him there's street Grand Prix in Delhi. He replies, "only in odd years." Benaud hasn't lost sense of humour.

Make Modi Luft flight to Calcutta. Fall asleep, woken by Max Kruger (Nine's statistician). "Which way do you think we are going?" I reply, "Forward, I hope." Wrong.

Pity, almost made Calcutta, but airport fog. Headed back to Delhi, technically correct — plane is going forward. Time in Delhi to contemplate take off to fog bound airport. Try again, pilot apologises, wasn't told of fog. Reach Calcutta 13:30 (they've converted me to airline speak), miss connection. Re-book: Delhi-Bhubaneshwar-Nagpur-Hyderabad; depart 17:30. Straightforward flight to Boobs (for short), but spend 90 minutes on tarmac. No parking bay, no communication with ground staff. Boobs to Nagpur, America's Cup leg, now tacking to Hyderabad, but chicken tikka and mint sauce dinner good.

Nags to Hyder uneventful. Arrive midnight, airport hotel 00:30, wake up call 05:30. Taxi to airport, 07:30, flt to Vizag leaves 07:45, arrives 1 hour later. Leave bags for someone to collect, taxi to ground, arrive 09:15. Australia batting 0/12, in fourth over, game started at 09:00. Michael Slater and Tim Gilbert doing commentary.

In either discomfort or tranquillity, that is an adventure.

Scoreboard

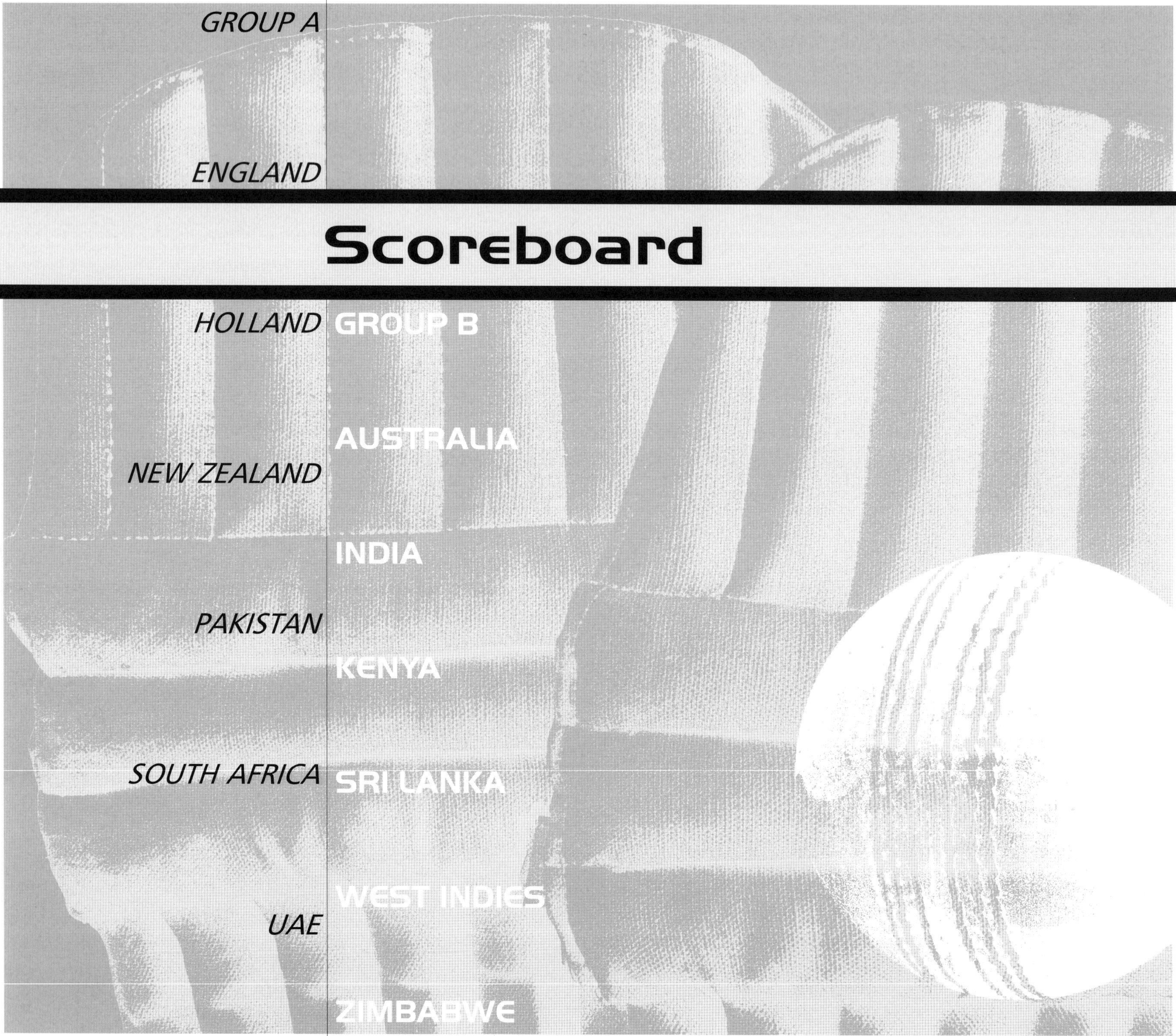

GROUP A

ENGLAND

HOLLAND

NEW ZEALAND

PAKISTAN

SOUTH AFRICA

UAE

GROUP B

AUSTRALIA

INDIA

KENYA

SRI LANKA

WEST INDIES

ZIMBABWE

Wills World Cup 1996

Match Venues Feb 14,1996 to March 17,1996

Peshawar ●
Rawalpindi ●

Gujranwala ●
Faisalabad ● ●
Lahore ●

● Chandigarh

CHINA

PAKISTAN

● Delhi

NEPAL

Jaipur ●

Gwalior ● ● Kanpur

● Patna

Karachi ●

BANGLADESH

INDIA

● Ahmedabad

● Vadodara

● Calcutta

● Nagpur

Cuttack ●

Bombay ●
(Mumbai) ● Pune

● Hyderabad   ● Vishakhapatnam

● Madras
Bangalore ● (Chennai)

● Kandy
Colombo ●   **SRI LANKA**

Source: Survey of India Maps and State Govt. Publications

INDIAN OCEAN

The Preliminary Matches GROUP A

HYDERABAD
West Indies beat Zimbabwe by six wickets
Zimbabwe 151 Ambrose 3 for 28
West Indies 155 for 4 in 29.3 overs, Campbell 47,
Lara 43 n.o.

CUTTACK
India beat Kenya by seven wickets
Kenya 199 Tikolo 65, Kumble 3 for 28
India 203 for 3 in 45.1 overs, Tendulkar 127, Jadeja 53

COLOMBO
Sri Lanka beat Zimbabwe by six wickets
Zimbabwe 228 Campbell 75, Vaas 2 for 30
Sri Lanka 229 for 4 in 37 overs, De Silva 91, Gurusinha 87

GWALIOR
India beat West Indies by five wickets
West Indies 173 Richardson 47, Kumble 3 for 35
India 174 for 6 Tendulkar 70

VISHAKHAPATNAM
Australia beat Kenya by 96 runs
Australia 304 M. Waugh 130, S. Waugh 82
Kenya 207 Otieno 85, Odumbe 50, Reiffel 2 for 18

PATNA
Zimbabwe beat Kenya by five wickets
Kenya 134 Strang 5 for 21
Zimbabwe 137 for 5 in 42.2 overs, Flower 45

BOMBAY (MUMBAI)
Australia beat India by 16 runs
Australia 258 M. Waugh 126, Taylor 59
India 242 in 48 overs, Tendulkar 90, Manjrekar 62,
Fleming 5 for 36

PUNE
Kenya beat West Indies by 73 runs
Kenya 166
West Indies 93

NAGPUR
Australia beat Zimbabwe by eight wickets
Zimbabwe 154 Warne 4 for 34
Australia 158 for 2 in 36 overs, M. Waugh 76 n.o.

DELHI
Sri Lanka beat India by six wickets
India 271 for 3 Tendulkar 137, Azharuddin 72
Sri Lanka 272 for 4 in 48.4 overs, Jayasuriya 79,
Tillekeratne 70 n.o.

JAIPUR
West Indies beat Australia by four wickets
Australia 229 Ponting 102, S. Waugh 57
West Indies 232 for 6 in 48.5 overs, Richardson 93 n.o.,
Lara 60

KANPUR
India beat Zimbabwe by 40 runs
India 247 for 5 Kambli 106, Sidhu 80
Zimbabwe 207 Raju 3 for 30

KANDY
Sri Lanka beat Kenya by 144 runs
Sri Lanka 398 for 5 De Silva 145, Gurusinha 84,
Ranatunga 75 n.o.
Kenya 254 for 7 Tikolo 96

The Preliminary Matches GROUP B

AHMEDABAD
New Zealand beat England by 11 runs
New Zealand 239 for 6 Astle 101
England 228 for 9 Hick 85

RAWALPINDI
South Africa beat UAE by 169 runs
South Africa 321 Kirsten 188, Cronje 57
UAE 152 for 8 Donald 3 for 21

VADODARA
New Zealand beat Holland by 119 runs
New Zealand 307 Spearman 68, Fleming 66, Cairns 52,
Parore 55
Holland 188 for 7 Harris 3 for 24

PESHAWAR
England beat UAE by eight wickets
UAE 136 Smith 3 for 29
England 140 for 2 in 35 overs, Thorpe 44 not out

FAISALABAD
South Africa beat New Zealand by five wickets
New Zealand 177 Donald 3 for 43
South Africa 178 for 5 in 37.3 overs, Cronje 78

PESHAWAR
England beat Holland by 49 runs
England 279 Hick 104, Thorpe 89
Holland 230 for 6 Van Noortwijk 64, Zuiderent 54

GUJRANWALA
Pakistan beat UAE by nine wickets
UAE 109 Mushtaq Ahmed 3 for 16
Pakistan 112 for 1 in 18 overs, Anwar 40 not out

RAWALPINDI
South Africa beat England by 78 runs
South Africa 230 Rhodes 37, Martin 3 for 33
England 153 Thorpe 46

LAHORE
Pakistan beat Holland by eight wickets
Holland 145 for 7 Waqar Younis 4 for 26
Pakistan 151 for 2 in 30.4 overs, Anwar 83 not out

FAISALABAD
New Zealand beat UAE by 109 runs
New Zealand 276 Twose 92, Spearman 78
UAE 167 for 9 Samerasekera 47 not out, Thomson 3 for 20

KARACHI
South Africa beat Pakistan by five wickets
Pakistan 242 for 6 Sohail 111
South Africa 243 for 5 Cullinan 65

LAHORE
UAE beat Holland by seven wickets
Holland 216 for 9 Cantrell 4, Aponso 45,
Dukhanwala 5 for 29
UAE 220 for 3 in 44.2 overs, Raza 84,
Mohammad 51 not out

KARACHI
Pakistan beat England by seven wickets
England 249 Smith 75, Atherton 66, Thorpe 52 not out
Pakistan 250 for 3 in 47.4 overs, Anwar 71, Ijaz 70,
Inzaman 53 not out

RAWALPINDI
South Africa beat Holland by 160 runs
South Africa 328 Hudson 161, Kirsten 83
Holland 168 Donald 2 for 21, Symcox 2 for 22

LAHORE
Pakistan beat New Zealand by 46 runs
Pakistan 281 for 5 Anwar 62, Sohail 50
New Zealand 235

The Quarter Finals

England vs Sri Lanka

Faisalabad, March 9, 1996. Toss: England
Result: Sri Lanka won by five wickets. Man of the Match: Sanath Jayasuriya

ENGLAND

R.A. Smith	run out	25
M.A. Atherton	c Kaluwitharana b Vaas	22
G.A. Hick	c Ranatunga b Muralitharan	8
G.P. Thopre	b Dharmasena	14
P.A. DeFreitas	lbw-b Jayasuriya	67
A.J. Steward	b Muralitharan	17
R.J. Russell	b Dharmasena	9
D.A. Reeve	b Jayasuriya	35
D.Gough	not out	26
P.J. Martin	not out	0
Extras	(lb 8, w 4)	12
Total	(eight wickets in 50 overs)	235

FALL OF WICKETS
1/31, 2/58, 3/66, 4/94, 5/145, 6/171, 7/173, 8/235

SRI LANKA BOWLING

Wickremasinghe 7-0-43-0	**Vaas** 8-1-29-1
Muralitharan 10-1-37-2	**Dharmasena** 10-0-30-2
Jayasuriya 9-0-46-2	**De Silva** 6-0-42-0

SRI LANKA

S.T. Jayasuriya	st Russell b Reeve	82
R.S. Kaluwitharanan	b Illingworth	8
A.P. Gurusinha	run out	45
P.A. De Silva	c Smith b Hick	31
A. Ranatunga	lbw-b Gough	25
H.P. Tillekeratne	not out	19
R.S. Mahanama	not out	22
Extras	(lb 1, w 2, nb 1)	4
Total	(five wickets in 40.4 overs)	236

FALL OF WICKETS
1/12, 2/113, 3/165, 4/194, 5/198

ENGLAND BOWLING

Martin 9-1-141-0	**Illingworth** 10-1-72-1	**Gough** 10-1-36-1
DeFreitas 3.4-0-38-0	**Reeve** 4-1-14-1	**Hick** 4-0-34-1

India vs Pakistan

Bangalore, March 9, 1996 (day/night). Toss: India
Result: India won by 39 runs. Man of the Match: N S Sidhu

INDIA

N.S. Sidhu	b Mushtaq	93
S.R. Tendulkar	b Ata-ur-Rehman	31
S.V. Manjrekar	c Miandad b Sohil	20
M. Azharuddin	c Latif b Younis	27
V.G. Kambli	b Mushtaq	24
A.D. Jadeja	c Sohail b Yunis	45
N.R. Mongia	run out	3
A. Kumble	c Miandad b Aqib	10
J. Srinath	not out	12
B.K.V. Prasad	not out	0
Extras	(lb 3, w 15, nb 4)	22
Total	(eight wkts in 50 overs)	287

Fall of Wickets
1/90, 2/138, 3/168, 4/200, 5/226, 6/236, 7/260, 8/279

PAKISTAN BOWLING

Younis 10-1-67-2	**Aquib** 10-0-67-1	**Ata-ur-Rehman** 10-0-40-1
Mushtaq 10-0-56-2	**Sohail** 5-0-39-1	**Malik** 5-0-25-0

PAKISTAN

Aamir Sohail	b Prasad	55
Saeed Anwar	c Kumble b Srinath	48
Ijaz Ahmed	c Srinath b Prasad	12
Inzamam-ul-Haq	c Mongia b Prasad	12
Salim Malik	lbw-b Kumble	38
Javed Miandad	run out	38
Rashid Latif	St Mongia b Raju	26
Mushtaq Ahmed	c and b Kumble	0
Waqar Younis	not out	4
Ata-ur-Rehman	lbw-b Kumble	0
Aqib Javed	not out	6
Extras	(b 1, lb 3, w 5)	9
Total	(nine wkts in 49 overs)	248

FALL OF WICKETS
1-84, 2-113, 3-122, 4-132, 5-184, 6-231,7-232, 8-239, 9-239

INDIA BOWLING

Srinath 9-0-61-1	**Prasad** 10-0-45-3	**Kumble** 10-0-48-3
Raju 10-0-46-1	**Tendulkar** 5-0-25-0	**Jadeja** 5-0-19-0

The Quarter Finals

South Africa vs West Indies

Karachi, March 11, 1996. Toss: West Indies
Result: West Indies won by 19 runs. Man of the Match: Brian Lara

WEST INDIES

S. Chanderpaul	c Cullinan b McMillan	**56**
C.O. Browne	c Cullinan b Matthews	**26**
B.C. Lara	c Pollock b Symcox	**111**
R.B. Richardson	c Kirsten b Symcox	**10**
R.A. Harper	lbw b McMillan	**9**
R.I.C. Holder	run out	**5**
K.L.T. Arthurton	c Hudson b Adams	**1**
J.C. Adams	not out	**13**
I.R. Bishop	b Adams	**17**
C.E.L. Ambrose	not out	**0**
Extras	(b 2, lb 11, w 2, nb 1)	**16**
Total	(eight wickets in 50 overs)	**264**

FALL OF WICKETS
1/42, 2/180, 3/210, 4/214, 5/227, 6/230, 7/230, 8/254

SOUTH AFRICA BOWLING

Pollock 9-0-46-0	**Matthews** 10-0-42-1	**Cronje** 3-0-17-0
McMillan 10-1-37-2	**Symcox** 10-0-64-2	**Adams** 8-0-45-2

SOUTH AFRICA

A.C.Hudson	c Walsh b Adams	**54**
G. Kirsten	hit wkt b Ambrose	**3**
D.J. Cullinan	c Bishop b Adams	**69**
W.J. Cronje	c Arthurton b Adams	**40**
J.N. Rhodes	c Adams b Harper	**13**
B.M. McMillan	lbw b Harper	**6**
S.M. Pollock	c Adams b Harper	**6**
S.J. Palframan	c & b Harper	**1**
P.L. Symcox	c Harper b Arthurton	**24**
C.R. Matthews	not out	**8**
P.R. Adams	b Walsh	**10**
Extras	(b 1, lb 4, w 2 , nb 4)	**11**
Total	(in 49.3 overs)	**245**

FALL OF WICKETS
1/21, 2/118, 3/140, 4/186, 5/196, 6/196, 7/198, 8/227, 9/228

WEST INDIES BOWLING

Ambrose 10-0-29-1	**Walsh** 8.3-0-49-1	**Bishop** 5-0-34-0
Harper 10-0-47-4	**Adams** 10-0-52-3	**Arthurton** 6-0-29-1

Australia vs New Zealand

Madras, March 11, 1996 (day/night). Toss: New Zealand
Result: Australia won by six wickets. Man of the Match: Mark Waugh

NEW ZEALAND

C.M. Spearman	c Healy b Reiffel	**13**
N.J. Astle	c Healy b Fleming	**1**
L.K. Germon	c Fleming b McGrath	**89**
S.P. Fleming	c S. Waugh b McGrath	**8**
C.Z. Harris	c Reiffel b Warne	**130**
R.G. Twose	b Bevan	**4**
C.L. Cairns	c Reiffel b M. Waugh	**4**
A.C. Parore	lbw b Warne	**11**
S.A. Thomson	run out	**11**
D.N. Patel	not out	**3**
Extras	(lb 6, w 3, nb 3)	**12**
Total	(nine wickets in 50 overs)	**286**

FALL OF WICKETS
1-15, 2-16, 3-44, 4-212, 5-227, 6-240, 7-259, 8-282, 9-286

AUSTRALIA BOWLING

Reiffel 4-0-38-1	**Fleming** 5-1-20-1	**McGrath** 9-2-50-2
M. Waugh 8-0-43-1	**S. Waugh** 4-0-25-0	**Bevan** 10-2-52-1

AUSTRALIA

M.A. Taylor	c Germon b Patel	**10**
M.E. Waugh	c Parore b Nash	**110**
R.T. Ponting	c sub (Kennedy) b Thomson	**31**
S.K. Warne	lbw b Astle	**24**
S.R. Waugh	not out	**59**
S.G. Law	not out	**42**
Extras	(b 1, lb 6, w 3, nb 3)	**13**
Total	(Four wickets in 47.5 overs)	**289**

FALL OF WICKETS:
1/19, 2/84, 3/127, 4/213

NEW ZEALAND BOWLING

Nash 9-1-44-1	**Patel** 8-0-45-1	**Cairns** 6.5-0-51-0
Harris 10-1-41-0	**Thomson** 8-0-57-1	**Astle** 3-0-21-1
Twose 3-0-23-0		

The Semi Finals

India vs Sri Lanka

Calcutta, March 13, 1996 (day/night). Toss: India
Result: Sri Lanka won by default. Man of the Match: Arvinda De Silva

SRI LANKA

S.T. Jayasuriya	c Prasad b Srinath	**1**
R.S. Kaluwitharana	c Manjrekar b Srinath	**0**
A.P. Gurusinha	c Kumble b Srinath	**1**
P.A. de Silva	b Kumble	**66**
R.S. Mahanama	retired hurt	**58**
A. Ranatunga	lbw b Tendulkar	**35**
H.P. Tillekeratne	c Tendulkar b Prasad	**32**
H.D.P.K. Dharmasena	b Tendulkar	**9**
W.P.U.J.C. Vaas	run out	**23**
G.P. Wickremasinghe	not out	**4**
M. Muralitharan	not out	**5**
Extras	(b 1, lb 10, w 4, nb 2)	**17**
Total	(eight wickets in 50 overs)	**251**

FALL OF WICKETS
1-1, 2-1, 3-35, 4-85, 5-168, 6-206, 7-236, 8-244.

INDIAN BOWLING

Srinath 7-1-34-3   **Kumble** 10-0-51-1   **Prasad** 8-0-50-1
Kapoor 10-0-40-0   **Jadeja** 5-0-31-0   **Tendulkar** 10-1-34-2

INDIA

S.R. Tendulkar	st Kaluwitharana b Jayasuriya	**65**
N.S. Sidhu	c Jayasuriya b Vaas	**3**
S.V. Manjrekar	b Jayasuriya	**25**
M.A. Azharuddin	c & b Dharmasena	**0**
V.G. Kambli	not out	**10**
J. Srinath	run out	**6**
A.D. Jadeja	b Jayasuriya	**0**
N.R. Mongia	c Jayasuriya b de Silva	**1**
A.R. Kapoor	c de Silva b Muralitharan	**0**
A. Kumble	not out	**0**
Extras	(lb 5, w 5)	**10**
Total	(eight wickets in 34.1 overs)	**120**

FALL OF WICKETS
1/8, 2/98, 3/99, 4/101, 5/110, 6/115, 7/120, 8/120

SRI LANKA BOWLING

Wickremasinghe 5-0-24-0   **Vaas** 6-1-23-1   **Dharmasena** 7-0-24-1
Muralitharan 7.1-0-29-1   **Jayasuriya** 7-1-12-3   **De Silva** 2-0-3-1

Australia vs West Indies

Mohali, March 14, 1996 (day/night). Toss: Australia
Result: Australia won by 5 runs. Man of the Match: Shane Warne

AUSTRALIA

M.E. Waugh	lbw b Ambrose	**0**
M.A. Taylor	b Bishop	**1**
R.T. Ponting	lbw b Ambrose	**0**
S.R. Waugh	b Bishop	**3**
S.G. Law	run out	**72**
M.G. Bevan	c Richardson b Harper	**69**
I.A. Healy	run out	**31**
P.R. Reiffel	run out	**7**
S.K. Warne	not out	**6**
Extras	(lb 11, w 5, nb 2)	**18**
Total	(eight wickets in 50 overs)	**207**

FALL OF WICKETS
1/0, 2/7, 3/8, 4/15, 5/153, 6/171, 7/186, 8/207

WEST INDIES BOWLING

Ambrose 10-1-26-2   **Bishop** 10-1-35-2   **Walsh** 10-1-33-0
Gibson 2-0-13-0   **Harper** 9-0-47-1   **Adams** 9-0-42-0

WEST INDIES

S. Chanderpaul	c Fleming b McGrath	**80**
C.O. Browne	c & b Warne	**10**
B.C. Lara	b S.Waugh	**45**
R.B. Richardson	not out	**49**
R.A. Harper	lbw b McGrath	**2**
O.D. Gibson	c Healy b Warne	**1**
J.C. Adams	lbw b Warne	**2**
K.L.T. Arthurton	c Healy b Fleming	**0**
I.R. Bishop	lbw b Warne	**3**
C.E.L. Ambrose	run out	**2**
C.A. Walsh	b Fleming	**0**
Extras	(lb 4, w 2, nb 2)	**8**
Total	(in 49.3 overs)	**202**

FALL OF WICKETS
1/25, 2/93, 3/165, 4/173, 5/178, 6/183, 7/187, 8/197, 9/202

AUSTRALIA BOWLING

McGrath 10-2-30-2   **Fleming** 8.3-0-48-2   **Warne** 9-0-36-4
M.Waugh 4-0-16-0   **S.Waugh** 7-0-30-1   **Reiffel** 5-0-13-0
Bevan 4-0-12-0   **Law** 2-0-13-0

The Final

Sri Lanka vs Australia

March 17, 1996 (day/night) Toss: Sri Lanka.
Result: Sri Lanka won by 7 wickets. Man of the Match: Aravinda de Silva.

AUSTRALIA

M.A. Taylor	c Jayasuriya b de Silva	**74**
M.E. Waugh	c Jayasuriya b Vaas	**12**
R.T. Ponting	b de Silva	**45**
S.R. Waugh	c de Silva b Dharmasena	**13**
S.K. Warne	st Kaluwitharana b Muralitharan	**2**
S.G. Law	c de Silva b Jayasuriya	**22**
M.G. Bevan	not out	**36**
I.A. Healy	b de Silva	**2**
P.R. Reiffel	not out	**13**
Extras	(b 10, w 11, nb 11)	**22**
Total	(seven wickets in 50 overs)	**241**

FALL OF WICKETS
1/36, 2/137, 3/152, 4/156, 5/170, 6/202, 7/205

SRI LANKA BOWLING

Wickremasinghe 7-0-38-0   Vaas 6-1-30-1
Muralitharan 10-0-31-1   Dharmasena 10-0-47-1
Jayasuriya 8-0-43-1   De Silva 9-0-42-3

SRI LANKA

S.T. Jayasuriya	run out	**9**
R.S. Kaluwitharana	c Bevan b Fleming	**6**
A.P. Gurusinha	b Reiffel	**65**
P.A. De Silva	not out	**107**
A. Ranatunga	not out	**47**
Extras	(lb 4, b 1, w 5, nb 1)	**11**
Total	(three wickets in 46.2 overs)	**245**

FALL OF WICKETS
1/12, 2/23, 3/148

AUSTRALIA BOWLING

McGrath 8.2-1-28-1   Fleming 6-0-43-1   Warne 10-0-58-0
Reiffel 10-0-49-1   M. Waugh 6-0-35-0   S. Waugh 3-0-15-0
Bevan 3-0-12-0

Top 10 Rankers

BATTING RECORDS

	M	I	N.O.	Runs	Ave	HS	100s	50s
S.R. Tendulkar (Ind)	7	7	1	523	87.17	137	2	3
M.E. Waugh (Aus)	7	7	1	484	80.67	130	3	1
P.A. De Silva (S.L.)	6	6	1	448	89.60	145	2	2
G. Kirsten (S.A.)	6	6	1	391	78.20	188*	1	1
Saeed Anwar (Pak)	6	6	2	329	82.25	83*	-	3
A.P. Gurusinha (S.L.)	6	6	-	307	51.17	87	-	3
W.J. Cronje (S.A.)	6	6	1	276	55.20	78	-	2
A.C. Hudson (S.A.)	4	4	-	275	68.75	161	1	1
Aamir Sohail (Pak)	6	6	-	272	45.33	111	1	2
B.C. Lara (W.I.)	6	6	1	269	53.80	111	1	1

BOWLING RECORDS

	M	Balls	Mds	Runs	Wkts	Avg	4WI	Best
A. Kumble (Ind)	7	418	3	280	15	18.67	-	3-28
Waqar Younis (Pak)	6	324	4	253	13	19.46	1	4-26
P. Strang (Zim)	5	253	4	192	12	16.00	2	5-21
R.A. Harper (W.I.)	6	348	6	219	12	18.25	1	4-47
D. Fleming (Aus)	6	272	3	221	12	18.42	1	5-36
S.K. Warne (Aus)	7	411	3	263	12	21.92	2	4-34
C.E.L. Ambrose (W.I.)	6	339	9	170	10	17.00	-	3-28
Mushtaq Ahmed (Pak)	6	342	2	238	10	23.80	-	3-16
Rajab Ali (Ken)	5	218	3	176	9	19.56	-	3-17
A. Donald (S.A.)	4	204	1	126	8	15.75	-	3-21

PHOTO CREDITS